W9-BHF-219

# PIVOT POINTS

# PIVOT POINTS

## A fragmented history of *Mental Health* in Saskatchewan

Jayne Melville Whyte

Bernadette Wagner, *Editor*

**Canadian Mental Health Association**
Saskatchewan

Copyright © CMHA (Sask) and Jayne Melville Whyte, 2012
Published by Canadian Mental Health Association (Saskatchewan Division) Inc.
2702 – 12<sup>th</sup> Avenue, Regina, Saskatchewan S4T 1J2
E-mail: contactus@cmhask.com
Phone: (306) 525-5601
Fax: (306) 569-3788

LIBRARY AND ARCHIVES CANADA
CATALOGUING IN PUBLICATION

Whyte, Jayne Melville,1947-.

Canadian Mental Health Association (Saskatchewan) Inc.

Pivot Points: A fragmented history of Mental Health in

Saskatchewan / Jayne Melville Whyte.

ISBN 978-0-9917109-0-4

1. Whyte, Jayne Melville, 1947-. 2. Wagner, Bernadette, 1962-. 3. Canadian Mental Health Association (Saskatchewan) Inc. 4. Mental Health- Saskatchewan – History. I. Title

Editor:  Bernadette Wagner

Cover art : *Biomorphic Swing,* Henry Peters

Author photo:  Brenda MacLauchlan

Book design: B-) Print Ink, Regina, Saskatchewan

Printing : Houghton Boston, Saskatoon, Saskatchewan

The conclusions and recommendations in this history are those of the author, and may not reflect the official position of the Canadian Mental Health Association (Saskatchewan Division) Inc., or of any persons or organizations that have contributed, financially or otherwise, to the production of this book.

Photocopying Permitted. Please acknowledge **Whyte, Jayne Melville,** *Pivot Points: A fragmented history of Mental Health in Saskatchewan.* **Regina: Canadian Mental Health Association Saskatchewan Inc., 2012.**

# ACKNOWLEDGEMENTS

The Canadian Mental Health Association (Saskatchewan Division) Inc. has sponsored a series of research and writing projects that have been consolidated into this history.   Dave Nelson, Executive Director, managed these projects; Phyllis O'Connor, Assistant Director deserved special appreciation for setting up and maintaining the research files and records; Lynn Hill provided desktop publishing and other support over the years, and the Board, staff and volunteers offered ongoing hospitality and encouragement.

The Population Health Fund, Health Canada financed *Iceberg on the Horizon* (2004).   Partners in that project included Saskatchewan Seniors Mechanism, Seniors' Education Centre at the University of Regina (now the Life Long Learning Centre), the Registered Psychiatric Nurses Association of Saskatchewan   (RPNAS), and the Saskatoon Council on Aging.

Saskatchewan Tourism, Parks, Culture and Sport funded *Visiting the Mentally Ill: Volunteer Visitors at Saskatchewan Hospital, Weyburn 1950-1965* (2009). A version of *Visiting* appeared in a special de-institutionalization issue of the *Histoire Sociale/ Social History* journal XLIV: 88, November 2011 thanks to Erika Dyck, guest editor.[1]

Saskatchewan Parks and Recreation Association funded *Beyond Barriers – to Participation: Recreation For Older Adults With Mental Illness* (June 2010), *Setting Goals and Building Capacity: A Recovery Model for CMHA Social Recreation in Saskatchewan* (June 2011), and *The Beginnings of White Cross Centres in Saskatchewan* (June 2012).

CMHA allocated a portion of an unrestricted Eli Lilly grant for *A Fragmented History of Mental Health Services for Children and Youth in Saskatchewan* (November 2011). Sharon Russell, widow of Dr. Terry

Russell allowed extensive use of his outline and manuscript, *Growing Pains: The Development of Children's Mental Health Services in Saskatchewan.* She and Laura Carment offered useful responses to an earlier draft of the CMHA paper on Child and Youth Services. Thank you to all the people who responded through interviews, surveys and conversations in each of the projects.

The staff at the Saskatchewan Archives Board was particularly helpful especially since the files needed to be scanned to meet the requirements of the *Privacy Act* by removing references to particular patients.

Special appreciation to editor, Bernadette Wagner, who asked clarifying questions and smoothed out the prose from the various projects.

Thank you to key CMHA and community readers who reviewed the draft and made useful suggestions for accuracy and editing. All errors and omissions are the responsibility of the author. Readers who want to improve future editions may contact CMHA Saskatchewan with corrections and additional information.

## ABOUT THE AUTHOR

**Jayne Melville Whyte**, mental health advocate, uses her own experience as a consumer, and now as a senior, to gather information and share ideas for improving mental health for all citizens including those who are in recovery with mental illness. Jayne's consumer experience began in 1965 and she has been active in CMHA since 1975. She earned a B.A. (Psychology) from the University of Winnipeg in 1992. Jayne lives in Regina and is a frequent visitor to the Archives. She enjoys speaking to groups about her life and research.

## ABOUT THE EDITOR

**Bernadette Wagner** loves to play with words and language. Her poetry, fiction, and nonfiction are rooted in her love of land, commitment to grassroots activism and the spirit of the prairies. Her work has appeared in journals, anthologies, and magazines and on radio and cd, television and film, in schools, on stages, in the streets and on the web. Her collection of poetry, *This hot place* (Thistledown Press, 2010), received a nomination for the Saskatchewan First Book Award.

# CONTENTS

INTRODUCTION...................................................................9

ABOUT THE CANADIAN MENTAL HEALTH ASSOCIATION................................11

ABOUT MENTAL HEALTH AND MENTAL ILLNESS.......................................13

ABOUT THE NAMES FOR PEOPLE WHO LIVE WITH MENTAL ILLNESS.............15

SASKATCHEWAN HOSPITALS AT NORTH BATTLEFORD AND WEYBURN........17

CMHA SASKATCHEWAN BEGINNINGS.................................................23

VOLUNTEER VISITORS ...........................................................27

THE SASKATCHEWAN PLAN AND MEDICARE.......................................43

WHITE CROSS CENTRE BEGINNINGS..............................................49

GOVERNMENT SERVICES AND CMHA IN THE 1960'S................................63

CHILDREN AND YOUTH MENTAL HEALTH PROGRAM BEGINNINGS..............71

THE FORGOTTEN CONSTITUENTS..................................................83

CONSUMERS AND COALITIONS....................................................87

MORE PLANS FOR CHILD AND YOUTH SERVICES...................................103

ISSUES FOR AN AGING POPULATION..............................................111

SOCIAL RECREATION PROGRAMS IN SASKATCHEWAN 2011......................115

CHANGING TRENDS AND STRATEGIC DIRECTIONS...............................129

APPENDIX A: CMHA SASKATCHEWAN PRESIDENTS 1950 – 2012...................138

INDEX........................................................................139

ENDNOTES....................................................................143

# 8 PIVOT POINTS

# INTRODUCTION

Pivot points occur in the lives of individuals, families, organizations, communities, and even mental health systems and organizations. A pivot point may be a single event, or a series of events, that changes the direction of beliefs and actions. Pivot points may have positive or negative impacts. A history looks back at interactions that may, or may not, have created change. This history focuses on mental health services in Saskatchewan and the story of the Canadian Mental Health Association (Saskatchewan Division) Inc.

Personally, one of my pivot points came in 1983 with the launch of *The Forgotten Constituents*, a CMHA Task Force report on mental health services in Saskatchewan. I had seen my first psychiatrist 18 years earlier at University Hospital in Saskatoon. I had joined CMHA eight years earlier and been appointed to the Division Board. The chair of the Task Force was my first psychiatrist, Dr. Ian McDonald. The Task Force had heard from a few consumers and families and CMHA felt it was important to get a patient perspective for the panel that launched the report at the annual meeting. I was nervous because CMHA was asking me to change from my role as patient to a role as critic and advocate. At that point, few self-identified consumers were visible in CMHA. The CMHA Saskatchewan program director said that unless I served as a "patient user" on the panel, the speaker would be invited from the United States. I agreed because "*someone* needed to do it." Then I threw myself into the CMHA consumer movement. Twenty-eight years later, this history scanned the larger context of the people, government and CMHA in Saskatchewan from building the first mental hospital in North Battleford in 1912 to drafting mental health strategy in 2012.

People with mental illness needed help. This history recorded how people did their best with what they knew at the time. Professional mental health workers, volunteers, CMHA staff, politicians, civil servants, tal health workers, volunteers, CMHA staff, politicians, civil servants, families and consumers helped because "someone needed to do it." Different players acted with different motivations and measures. As a person who lives with a dissociative disorder, I know there are many ways to see and respond. One fragment may not understand the rationale and reactions of another fragment. But each has a good reason for the ideas and actions.

Research clarified some of the context and the conditions. I suspect how much I've left out. No one sees the whole picture. But my hope is that this history shows pivot points when well-intentioned people tried to make life better for people with lived experience of mental illness. It may be your story too.

*Jayne Melville Whyte*

*September 2012*

# ABOUT THE CANADIAN MENTAL HEALTH ASSOCIATION

The Canadian Mental Health Association (CMHA), founded in 1918, was one of the oldest voluntary organizations in Canada. CMHA Saskatchewan, formed in 1950, was the first organized Division in Canada. In 2011, CMHA provided direct service to more than 100,000 Canadians through the combined efforts of more than 10,000 volunteers and staff in over 135 branches. As a nation-wide non-government organization (NGO), the Canadian Mental Health Association promoted the mental health of all Canadians and supported the resilience and recovery of people experiencing mental illness. CMHA accomplished this mission through advocacy, education, research, and service delivery. The website www.cmha.ca provided more information.

The Association operated at the National, Division (provincial/ territorial) and Branch (local community) levels. CMHA Saskatchewan worked as a community-based organization (CBO)[a] that supported and promoted the rights of persons with mental illness to maximize full potential; and promoted and enhanced the mental health and well being of all members of the community. In 2012, Saskatchewan had nine branches located in Regina, Saskatoon, Moose Jaw, Swift Current, Kindersley, Battlefords, Prince Albert, Weyburn, and Yorkton.

Over the years and in different publications, CMHA's name appeared in different forms, as the Mental Health Association in Saskatchewan and Saskatchewan Mental Health Association. Similar variations occurred in the designation of the national CMHA. For this paper the format has been standardized as CMHA National, with CMHA Saskatchewan denoting the provincial Division, and CMHA Branch with the community name. CMHA often refers to itself as the Association. During its history it has self-identified as a voluntary organization to recognize the importance of its volunteers, as an NGO to differentiate

---

a    All acronyms in the Index include complete name.

from government mental health services, and as a Community Based Organization (CBO) to identify with the community it serves.

# ABOUT MENTAL HEALTH AND MENTAL ILLNESS

Mental health is as important as physical health. The World Health Organization defined health as "a state of complete physical, mental and social well-being and not merely the absence of disease or infirmity." Mental health is the capacity of individuals to interact with one another and their environment in ways that enhance or promote their sense of well-being; their sense of control and choice with their life; optimal use of their mental abilities; achievement of their own goals (both personal and collective); and their quality of life. Recovery is a way of living a satisfying, hopeful and productive life even with the limitations created by the illness.

Mental illness refers to specific, diagnosed disorders such as schizophrenia, mood (depression and bi-polar) disorders, anxiety (panic, phobias, obsessive compulsive) disorders, and other psychiatric diagnoses. People who live with mental disorders can enjoy good mental health and balance the social, physical, spiritual, economic and emotional aspects of life with a choice of appropriate and effective community and health resources.

# ABOUT THE NAMES FOR PEOPLE WHO LIVE WITH MENTAL ILLNESS

The words used to identify and self-identify as *persons with lived experience of mental illness* changed over the years. Some people chose to be called *consumers* of mental health service because consumers expected choice and personal power in every aspect of survival, health, and enjoyment. The CMHA National definition in 1987 said, "Consumers are people with direct experience of significant mental health problems who have used the resources available from the mental health system."

Because service providers use the terms *patients* and *clients*, this perspective is reflected throughout this book. *Members* belong to the CMHA and/or to programs offered through CMHA, such as Regina members of The Club and Prince Albert members of The Nest, the local names for their drop-in centers. People who belong to independent self-help groups, for example Crocus Coop in Saskatoon, also refer to themselves as members. Self-help participants sometimes self-identify as *peers,* as in "peer-support" which recognizes, even celebrates, the identity and equality of persons who share a common experience. Other terms, like *survivors* and *thrivers,* self-identify stages and self-perceptions of living with mental illness.

The terms *person* and *people* recognizes their common identity with all individuals with strengths, abilities, dreams, needs and human value. The term *citizen* values basic human rights and civic responsibilities regardless of any difference or disability.

The Canadian Charter of Rights and Freedoms states that people can not be discriminated against because of disability, and requires society to provide the "accommodation and supports that enable people with psychiatric disability to lead safe, dignified lives in the community."[2]

CANADIAN CHARTER OF RIGHTS AND FREEDOMS

Equality Rights
Equality before and under law and equal protection and benefit of
law

15. (1) Every individual is equal before and under the law and has
the right to the equal protection and equal benefit of the law without
discrimination and, in particular, without discrimination based on
race, national or ethnic origin, colour, religion, sex, age or mental
or physical disability.

Affirmative action programs

(2) Subsection (1) does not preclude any law, program or activity
that has as its object the amelioration of conditions of
disadvantaged individuals or groups including those that are
disadvantaged because of race, national or ethnic origin, colour,
religion, sex, age or mental or physical disability.

*Persons with lived experience* or *persons with direct experience of mental illness* reflects the language chosen by the Mental Health Commission of Canada. *Persons with lived experience* recognizes that family members also live with the impact of mental illness. In this history, *consumers* designate people who live with mental illness and seek help in the mental health system. *People with mental health problems* recognizes that many people who need help do not access the fragmented resources.

# SASKATCHEWAN HOSPITALS AT NORTH BATTLEFORD AND WEYBURN

Before Saskatchewan became a province in 1905, people[3] with mental illness who were a danger to themselves or others, or an excessive burden to their families and neighbours, could be taken before a judge or magistrate. The judge could order that the person be incarcerated in Stony Mountain Prison or the Brandon Mental Asylum in Manitoba. That often meant a life sentence of custodial care. Mentally disordered persons (as they were then called) were usually *not* released back to their home and community.

*Staff Cottages at SHNB CIRCA 1930 Saskatchewan Archives Board R-PS 59-431-01*

The question of mental hygiene and a mental asylum arose early in the legislature of the new Saskatchewan assembly. In 1907, Premier Walter Scott asked the provincial health officer, Dr. David Low, to visit mental hospitals in eastern Canada and the United States. Low recommended a collection of cottages with staff and small groups of 10 to 20 patients. Toronto psychiatrist, Dr. C. K. Clarke, admitted that small family style treatment cottages "gives ideal conditions for the patients themselves" but advised against the plan "for both economic and climatic reasons."[4]

Saskatchewan Hospital North Battleford  (SHNB) with an estimated capacity of one thousand patients opened in 1914. Dr. James Walter MacNeill, the first Superintendent from 1914 until 1945, changed the name from 'asylum' to 'hospital' and insisted that patients be treated as human beings who needed help with their illness.[5] The doctors lived in cottages on the grounds.

The North Battleford hospital soon reached capacity. When Saskatchewan Hospital Weyburn (SHW) opened in December 1921, its first patients moved from North Battleford including 78 persons who had been in mental hospitals since birth. Six months later, two-thirds of Weyburn's 900 beds were full. A staff of 60 nurses (female) and 60 attendants (male) cared for over 600 patients.[6] The hospital provided custodial care. Cold water baths and wet sheet wraps calmed disturbed patients in the days before tranquilizers and anti-depressants. The main treatments were water and work.

*SHW Aerial View 1959*
*Saskatchewan Archives Board PS-59-431-01*

Patient labour was essential for the operation of the hospitals. In preparation for the opening of the second hospital, patients in the sewing rooms of SHNB turned huge bolts of cotton into bedding and uniforms for the new SHW. Patients also made hair mattresses for the beds. Weyburn patients cut willows along the Souris River and wove chairs and other furniture for the lawns and sitting rooms. That furniture was used and renewed until the mid-1950s.

Patients worked all over the hospital: kitchen, laundry, sewing room, tailor shop, shoemaker, mattress and upholstery shop, grounds keeping, power and filtration plants, carpentry, paint shop, tinsmith, and maintenance departments. Many patients tended the farms that surrounded both Saskatchewan Hospitals. Work crews looked after the fields, dairy, pigs, poultry and gardens that provided much of the food for the institutions. At Weyburn, from 1921 to the mid-fifties, patients did the housekeeping under the supervision of nursing staff. In 1955 when two scrub machines were purchased to wash and wax the floors, patients helped move furniture and carried the clean and dirty water to and from the machines. In 1957 the hospital hired a head housekeeper and seven staff.

The Weyburn grounds were beautifully landscaped until the late 1950's when the front flower bed became a parking lot and a new attitude in administration reduced the role of patients as unpaid labour. Although patients still worked in many departments, their activities were called occupational therapy (OT) or work experience in preparation for discharge into the community.

Work provided exercise and activity. Patients, in groups as large as 200, walked on the grounds. In the Admissions Ward, newly admitted patients were actively treated and OT played an important role in keeping them busy and stimulated until they either got better or were assigned to long-term wards. On the long-term wards, if patients did not work, they sat in chairs or walked in the halls all day.

In 1929, Saskatchewan Department of Public Health invited a team from the National Committee for Mental Hygiene to inspect the hospitals. Dr. Clarence Hincks and nurse Marjorie Keyes suggested reforms for the mental hospitals, but also for mental health programs for children and youth in schools, and for the general public. The Hincks report warned that without preventive measures, 4% of children would require psychiatric treatment in their lifetime.[7] The same report commended the OT program at North Battleford Provincial Hospital under the direction of matron Miss Hazel Jaques and her staff; patients' crafts won prizes at community exhibitions and fairs and were known throughout Saskatchewan.[8] Hincks' recommendation for mental health clinics and psychiatric wards in general hospitals led to the creation of the Munroe Wing at the Regina General Hospital. Depression, drought and World War II delayed implementation of other recommendations regarding research and the separation of people with mental retardation from the patients with mental illness.

By the time Hincks completed a second evaluation in 1945, the combined population of the two mental hospitals had doubled from 2,000 to 4,000 and Saskatchewan led the nation in the number of mental hospital deaths per capita.[9]

In 1930 and again in 1945, Hincks proposed community services for both adults and children. He recommended mental hygiene clinics in Saskatoon and Regina and traveling clinics to six other cities and towns. He proposed that clinic personnel monitor patients, provide mental hy-

giene training for health, education and welfare workers in the communities, and offer guidance for children with emotional and behavioural problems.   Hincks advised again in 1945 that mental defectives[b]
be removed from the Weyburn Hospital to a suitably constructed institution.  The 1945 report of the National Committee on Mental Hygiene
also recommended sterilization of the mentally ill and mental defectives,
especially girls and women.  The sterilization idea was not sanctioned in
Saskatchewan.[10]

The mental hospitals in North Battleford and Weyburn formed their
own communities.  Staff members were more connected to the hospital
than to the neighbouring city and often suffered the stigma associated
with their patients.  For recreation, the hospital workers including doctors, student attendants (male), and student nurses (female) formed
teams for recreation including curling, ball games, hockey, dances and
card parties.

Nurses and attendants worked 12-hour shifts with one day off per
week.  Duty schedules lengthened on patient dance evenings.  Segreg-
ated male and female wards, and a policy that patients were not allowed
to dance with each other, meant that hospital personnel were expected to
dance with patients of the opposite sex.  After the dance, the day shift returned to the ward with the patients and helped them get ready for bed.
Movie evenings also extended working days (without extra pay).   In
1946, staff negotiated a 48-hour week.  To create a professional workforce that could offer treatment as well as custodial care, in 1947 the
Psychiatric Services Branch (PSB) started the psychiatric nursing program to train existing staff at the hospitals at North Battleford and Weyburn, and recruited students from local communities and even from other
countries.[11]

In 1945 Dr. D. G. McKerracher followed MacNeill as director of
SHNB and provincial commissioner of Psychiatric Services.  In 1951 Dr.
Abram Hoffer became provincial director of the psychiatric research
program.  The new Superintendent for SHW, Dr. Humphrey Osmond,
was interested in research into the best conditions and treatments for

---

b    This term was used before *mentally retarded,* or *intellectual, cognitive and devel-
    opmental handicaps* or Downs' Syndrome. The mental hospital provided custodial
    care for children who grew into adults with disabilities still housed in the institu-
    tion.

people with psychiatric disorders.   Notably, Osmond and Hoffer re-searched with LSD to understand and treat mental illness and alcohol-ism.[12]   Along with architect, Kiyo Izumi, they planned hospitals with small wards of about 10 patients that paid attention to the distorted per-ceptions of space and design that affected patients with schizophrenia.[13]

These doctors and hospital administrators were disturbed that the mental hospitals had become a dumping ground.   Some patients did not necessarily need medical or psychiatric treatment including vagrants (today's term might be 'homeless'), old people and children without anyone to care for them, characters who did not easily fit into society, and children with mental handicaps.   But the doctors were also govern-ment employees.   The professionals, in consultation with the politicians of the time, realized that until conditions in the mental hospitals were brought to the attention of the public, there would be little political will to improve the lives of patients.   The National Committee for Mental Hygiene had investigated, on behalf of people with mental disorders, from a position outside either government or professional partiality.   In 1950, CMHA offered a vehicle for mobilizing public opinion and push-ing for improvements.

## CMHA SASKATCHEWAN BEGINNINGS

Mental illness and the search for wellness may be as old as humanity, but the CMHA history began with one American. Clifford Beers was sent to a mental hospital, and with the help of family and hospital staff, he recovered. He left hospital determined to make life better for people with mental illness. His book in 1908, *A Mind that Found Itself,* told the story of his institutionalization and recovery. The next year, Beers set up the first National Committee for Mental Hygiene in the United States to stimulate improved conditions in mental asylums.

In Ontario, Dr. Clarence M. Hincks, a psychiatrist with lived experience of mental illness, and Dr. C.K. Clarke, Dean of Medicine and Professor of Psychiatry at the University of Toronto followed Beers' work. After meeting him, they started the Canadian National Committee for Mental Hygiene, with 18 influential business and professional leaders on the Board of Directors. Board members agreed to pledge $1,000 per year for three years to get the organization launched. Drawing room meetings in Toronto and Montreal raised funds when wealthy women came to hear Clifford Beers share his story. They donated money for improved conditions in mental hospitals and for research into better treatments.

The Canadian National Committee for Mental Hygiene held its first official meeting in Ottawa on April 26, 1918. By fall, the Committee opened an office with Clarke as Medical Director and Hincks as Associate Medical Director. They hired Miss Dorothy Keyes, a graduate nurse with extra training in psychiatry, and two secretaries, Anne Abbott and Doris Secord.[14]

Clarke, Hincks, and Keyes conducted surveys of mental hospitals, the first at the invitation of the Manitoba government in 1918. Soon the team reported to the legislatures of most Canadian provinces. As described earlier, Hincks made two Saskatchewan visits, one in 1930 and one in 1945.

When the University of Saskatchewan in Saskatoon established a College of Education in 1928, two psychologists, Dr. Sam Laycock and Dr. Frank M. Quance, headed the new college.[15]  In 1929, Laycock served as the first educational psychologist with the Saskatoon School Board. He was instrumental in establishing the first class for retarded students, and in 1931, he initiated the first class for gifted students.  Laycock emphasized the importance of family, and encouraged strong links between families and schools. He became the first Saskatchewan President of the Home and School Association from 1938 to 1942.[16] In 1940, with J. D. M. Griffith, National Director of CMHA and W. Line of the University of Toronto, Laycock published a *Manual for Teachers: Mental Hygiene.*   In 1947, they developed a program "to train selected teachers to work in a liaison capacity between the home and school" with the goal of improving children's mental health.[17]  The College of Education graduated hundreds of teachers with the "mental health point of view" during the 1940s and 1950s.[18]  Laycock served on the Scientific Planning Committee of the National Committee for Mental Hygiene. He had been instrumental in beginning the CMHA Saskatoon branch. In 1950, he became the first president of the new Canadian Mental Health Association Division in Saskatchewan and a key member of the Division's Scientific Planning Committee.

White Cross Logo CMHA

By 1950, the National Committee on Mental Hygiene was in the midst of a re-organization. The name changed to the Canadian Mental Health Association. The White Cross logo implied the parallel of mental health with the physical health represented by the familiar Red Cross. A proposed grey cross suggested that no one is totally well or totally ill, but the CMHA National board chose the White Cross. [19]

On November 27, 1950, the National Board of Directors formally recognized Saskatchewan as the first provincial division of CMHA with Laycock as first President.   Funding came from the federal Department of Health and Welfare. Two other divisions, in New Brunswick and Nova Scotia, were not funded at that time.

Professionals and government members influenced the direction of CMHA Saskatchewan through the Scientific Planning Committee.

Policies and many other decisions requested or required their approval. The committee also allocated the CMHA Saskatchewan research grants. McKerracher, head of the re-organized Psychiatric Services Branch (PSB), Department of Public Health, chaired the CMHA committee. Other CMHA Board and/or Committee members working for government included the directors of the mental hospitals in North Battleford and Weyburn and the provincial director of psychiatric research.[20]

The 1952 CMHA National annual report set out six priorities: public education; service to the mentally disabled; surveys and social action; education and training of special groups; research; and international liaisons.[21] To improve conditions for mental patients required educating the public about existing situations while inspiring general confidence that better treatments meant care and cure. Influential women participated in the socialization of patients through the volunteer visiting program and took their plight to the public. Surveys of mental hospitals and prisons evaluated institutions and made recommendations for reform.

In the effort to raise community awareness, CMHA extended education and training to groups such as teachers, nurses, and clergy who acted as first points of contact for referrals to mental health services. The early researchers were optimistic that mental illness could be prevented and cured through lifestyle, diet, therapy and medication; both the national and division CMHA offered research grants. The CMHA National office established contacts in the United States and in Europe, attended conferences and corresponded with international colleagues.

The newly formed Saskatchewan Division reached out to towns, rural municipalities, and community organizations. Field representatives toured the province, publicized the needs of the mentally ill, raised funds, and conducted public education about good mental health. They attracted audiences with "moving pictures" from the National Film Board and other sources.

Each year a package of information went to churches and community groups, often the Home and School Association, throughout the province. Volunteers organized community gatherings and door-to-door canvassing on behalf of CMHA. Their literature highlighted its work to improve conditions in the mental hospitals and to fund research. The annual canvass raised much of the money needed for the operation of the provincial organization.

The 1958 report to the national annual meeting noted that Saskatchewan's campaign had sold 15,000 memberships and raised "nine cents per capita."[22]

## VOLUNTEER VISITORS

Volunteer Visiting was a major service in the early years of the CMHA Saskatchewan. [23] Visitors from Saskatoon, Prince Albert, Duck Lake and Shellbrook visited regularly at Saskatchewan Hospital North Battleford.[24] Trips from Regina every second week to Saskatchewan Hospital Weyburn began in May 1952 and continued into the 1960s. Occasionally the schedule changed because of special events and holidays, but rarely because of blizzards and adverse weather.

Dr. Osmond in a letter to CMHA in January 1960 recalled:

*... half a dozen ladies, headed by Mrs. R. J. Davidson, ... driven down by Mr. Art Riddell, then as now a keen supporter and hard worker for the C.M.H.A. That year the road was very rough and it was wet too so they often arrived spattered with mud. No one was much in favor of the volunteers – not even the C.M.H.A. who at that time were not greatly interested in mental hospitals – but the volunteers kept on coming. Most people thought they would stop before long but they didn't. Indeed they've gathered strength. We can still do with more volunteers but we are very pleased to be able to pay tribute to those who have done so much for us.[25]*

In a review of the volunteer program, written in 1961, Mrs. Agnes Davidson noted that the beginning program had its setbacks:

*It was in 1951 that the Scientific Planning Committee of C.M.H.A. felt that it would be a good thing if a visiting program could be started to the two Saskatchewan Hospitals and to Munroe Wing.*

*The first tentative effort was to send two visitors to Munroe Wing. At the time little was known about such a visiting program so that the visitors became discouraged and a visiting program was not established until sometime later at the Wing.*

*During the fall of 1951 the Health Committee of the Local Council of Women along with others studied some of the problems of the mentally ill. This was done under the leadership of Dr. Neil Agnew, at that time Executive Director of C.M.H.A. Saskatchewan Division. The committee as a whole felt that they were not ready to start such a program at that time, although they toured the [Weyburn] Hospital early in 1952.*

*Because of my dual commitment as a Board member of the Saskatchewan Division and as a committee member of the Health Committee, it seemed to me that a visiting group could be formed.*

Volunteer visiting started in 1952, the same year that Saskatchewan Hospital Weyburn (SHW) hired their first social worker, Mary Vogt, and their first research psychologist, Dr. Robert Sommer. The professionals designed a project to see what would happen if certain patients received the best possible treatment under the most favorable program. A "total push" program stimulated patients to be active.

The first volunteer visit encouraged the visitors and the staff at the Weyburn hospital regarding the value of the visiting program. Initially, neither patients nor visitors were quite sure what was happening.

*On entering the ward the gentleman accompanying us found chairs in the centre of the room and we, the fledgling visitors, looked around to see where to begin. The ward was not the cheerful place a similar ward is today nor were the visitors as attractively dressed.*

*An elderly woman half lay, half sat on a lounge and looked so woe begone that I felt I could not make matters worse so I approached her. She responded to my greeting and asked me to read from the Bible. We talked a little while together and as I moved away Mr. McKenzie came over to talk with her as for some time she had not communicated with the staff. This first visit was a momentous one for our team. We went fifteen more times during that year. Each time learning a little more about visiting the mentally ill.*

As they became more experienced, volunteers took more initiative in developing diversions for the patients. Food usually played an important part in any activity.

*After a great deal of consultation with staff members it was decided to give a picnic to a few patients selected by the staff. Because the day chosen proved unsuitable, the picnic was held in the balcony of the auditorium. The patients and the visitors spent a very happy time together and when it was time for the former to go back to their ward, they carried with them at their own request some of the goodies that were left over for their friends. This gesture of friendship did much to establish the visitors favourably in the eyes of the patients not only on 3C but other wards as well.*

As nineteen visitors went regularly each trip, private cars were not practical. CMHA chartered a bus from the Saskatchewan Transportation Company for the volunteers. Family members paid a nominal fee for transportation to visit relatives in hospital. The bus sometimes stopped in communities between Regina and Weyburn to pick up visitors. Over the course of the year in 1960, 243 relatives and 635 visitors traveled on the Charter

*Busload of Visitors at Weyburn 1950's*
*Saskatchewan Archives Board RA-25,040*

Bus to Weyburn. Following the Regina example, Saskatoon and Prince

Albert chartered buses for the monthly trips to North Battleford.

The visiting programs offered entertainment, socialization and friendship in the dreary routine of patients' lives but it required a high level of commitment from the volunteers. The same people tried to return regularly to get to know the people on the wards. The language team offered patients the opportunity to communicate in their first languages, a gift to the Ukrainians, Germans, Chinese and other nationalities confined to the hospital. Visitors played cards, shot pool, went bowling or started conversations. Parties and teas were special occasions with flowers for people celebrating birthdays that month. CMHA Saskatchewan organized Operation Friendship to collect Christmas presents from churches and service clubs that were distributed at the December visit or left with staff so that each patient had a package on Christmas morning.

A letter in September 1953 from Osmond to Davidson, President of Saskatchewan Division thanked the Regina Ladies for a picnic, recognized Mr. Art Lobb, the Executive Director, for the inauguration of the bus service and commended the "good roots" of the program. Osmond acknowledged the difficulties and disappointments in organizing and sustaining the program. He may have been referring to the broad picture of hospital conditions or some particular difficulty that Davidson had raised because he said, "The initial step is always that of recognizing that a problem exists; until that first step is taken there is nothing that can be done about it."

Osmond pioneered the idea that patients could take more responsibility for their lives and behaviour:

> We hope, before too long to have a patients society running, operated by the patients for the patients. I feel they should liaise with C.M.H.A. It would be an excellent piece of mental education and would establish the idea that the mentally sick can be as responsible and sensible as anyone else. Most of them can be, much of the time, if we only allow and encourage them to be.

Davidson and Osmond maintained a correspondence to refine and improve the visitors' program. An undated carbon copy titled *Women's Voluntary Services in Mental Hospitals* suggested a long list of "possible activities that might be carried out by volunteer women's groups" outside and inside the hospitals. Osmond listed the importance of the visitors as "a mental health lobby" about the needs of both in-patients and discharged patients. He appreciated the volunteers' part in collecting "comforts and supplies, clothing, furniture and Christmas presents." He suggested that "women with suitable skills and temperament" work with patients in the OT Department including special projects like a cooking shop. Volunteers brought old hats and jewelry and other supplies used in OT where patients made "saleable goods."

In addition to the socials and dances within the hospital, Osmond encouraged volunteer visitors to invite patients for walks, drives, and visits to the theatre. Even further, volunteers "could help with patient rehabilitation – finding jobs, living accommodation, develop interests, friendly support and advice." He advocated "taking people to their homes" though it is not clear whether that meant the patients' homes or the volunteer's home but he also asked for CMHA assistance in "boarding out experiences." In his list of possible tasks, Osmond invited evaluation: "They could note deficiencies in the hospital program and encourage the administration to improve conditions. … They could report favourably on aspects of the hospital deserving it."

The Volunteer Visitors took seriously their mandate to "note deficiencies." In 1953, a team of four women visited the female admitting ward, the senile ward, the mental defective ward, the basement wards, and the facilities for patients with tuberculosis (T.B.). Crowding was a major issue. In the Admitting Ward, the visitors noted a shortage of space and staff to accommodate insulin shock treatments. They also commented on other features:

*Also off the admitting ward is a small occupational therapy room. Interesting work is being done by about ten patients seated around a long table. Free movement around the room was impossible due to its small size. There was also a sitting room in connection with this ward. This whole ward was very pleasant and the physical surroundings were more agreeable than any of the others that we visited. There were fewer patients and the numbers limited to insure more intensive treatment.*

The four investigators inquired about the number of younger people in the Senile Ward. "We were told that some of the contributing factors were conditions today, lack of housing, lack of security, and many are not wanted by their families."

The Low Grade Defective Ward held 98 persons of all ages. Today the residents there would be called 'persons with developmental handicaps' or 'persons with learning disabilities' or diagnosed with Downs Syndrome:

> *We noted that they were affectionate and fairly happy. Two of the patients we saw had arm restraints. There appeared to be nothing for them to do and we were told they live their whole life on this ward. They never get outdoors.*

In the basement ward for the aged, bedridden and chronic patients, there were 106 residents. The ward had been repainted and the women noted bright curtains on the high windows. In the Refractory Ward, they "wondered how the cement floors could possibly be warm, especially in the solitary side rooms." Solitary rooms isolated patients who were violent or unruly (refractory) until they calmed down. For safety, there was no furniture in a solitary room.

The T.B. wards were in a separate building holding 46 female patients on the main floor and 56 male patients on the second floor.

> *The building was over-crowded and under-ventilated in the extreme. Along with mental illness, these patients have T.B. which is why they are isolated. ... The main thing that impressed us was the over-crowding and the impossibility of giving the intensive treatment to more patients. This treatment would give a chance to return a greater number to the community.*

In summarizing their survey, the team of volunteer visitors suggested that overcrowding might be reduced if some of the elderly people received care in nursing homes near their home community. They remarked on the cleanliness of all wards, but the lack of ventilation concerned them. "We ... were told that all ventilation ducts had been closed because of their fire hazard." And the final comment of the report had a handwritten note that said 'emphasize this': "With the exception of the parole ward, where patients could go out and in at will, no ward had access to the outdoors."

The Visitors showed the report to Dr. Ian Clancy, Clinical Director on a regular visiting day and then presented it at the Regina Council of Women annual meeting in January 1954. In 1955, an addition increased the capacity of the T.B. ward by fifty beds. The bowling alley in the basement of the new T.B. wing provided another recreation and exercise opportunity for staff and patients.[26]

The 1950's brought a number of improvements in the Occupational and Recreational Therapy Departments at Weyburn Hospital. Ray Belanger writing in the SHW history, *Under the Dome,* defined OT:

> *Occupational Therapy was described as any activity prescribed and professionally guided with purpose of aiding recovery by occupying the patient's body and mind. Occupational Therapy has existed as an important part of treatment in the hospital almost since its beginning.*[27]

In Weyburn Hospital in 1954, under the leadership of Earl Beck and Ken Pollock, Recreation Therapy staff included the two therapists and two nurses. Every student spent two months in the Recreation department. The emphasis changed from large group activities to concentration on the individual.

Recreation activities (to which the Volunteer Visitors contributed) included dances, bingos, card parties, and amateur nights, sing songs, ball games and skating. A small physiotherapy (PT) department provided what was called "medical gymnastics" for long-term patients. Supervisor of physiotherapy Mrs. M. Vint stated, "Patients of long standing illness, who had previously been considered resistant to any form of treatment, many consigned to a quasinegative existence, are aroused by P.T. from their morbid introspection."[28] The Volunteers organized the Family Day picnic each summer in an effort to invite families to visit.

Kay Parley, who wrote a semi-fictional book, *Lady with a Lantern,* about her experiences as a patient and then as student nurse at Weyburn, documented the range of recreation facilities available at the hospital:

*We had a small bowling alley, assembly hall with stage, balcony and motion picture projector, and we had ball diamonds, bowling lawns, tennis courts, skating and curling rinks. We had sports activities ranging from medicine balls to bikes. To expand our facilities and help in the re-socialization of patients, we had arrangements to take patients to a bowling alley, a movie theatre, and a public swimming pool down town.[29]*

Meanwhile the Wards where patients lived held 60 to 144 people in the same room. Beds were so close together that there was barely room to get between to tuck in the sheets in some wards. In some cases, only 12 inches separated the beds. The 1956 CMHA brief to the provincial government protested the under-staffing and overcrowding in SHW. Patients were crowded into one-third of the 100 square feet living space per patient recommended by 1950's hospital standards. The brief also noted that the American Psychiatric Association standards for adequate staffing had been adopted in Canada. The SHW was significantly below the guidelines for the number of nurses,

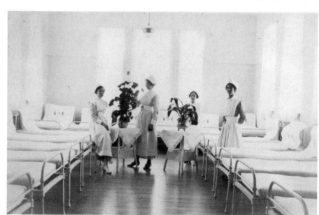

*Nurses in Ward at Weyburn 1958*
*Saskatchewan Archives Board-RA-6380.7*

doctors, psychologists and social workers for their population. Another comparison noted that in a general hospital the ratio was 1.3 staff per patient, while in the mental hospital the ratio was one staff for 3.4 patients.[30]

By 1957, the Hospital changed its approach to implement activities that prepared patients for discharge to group homes or their own homes. Some people had never left their wards for years. The Volunteer Visitors started a new initiative of bringing patients to Regina for the day.

*A new project this year was the entertaining of patients from Weyburn in the city for a day of sight seeing and attending a sporting event to a buffet supper in the Clubroom. Six such suppers were held with an average of 8 guests each. On one occasion, the guests were women. Delicious salads, pies and relishes were donated by the volunteers. Friends donated money to help with the project; otherwise any needed funds were from the volunteer account.*

For the first five years, the Recreation Department coordinated the Volunteer Visitors program and negotiated with individual wards under the direction of Superintendent Osmond. A 1957 letter from Osmond suggested that CMHA either hire a coordinator or "push the government to supply full time organizers", following the examples of similar programs in the United States.[31]   The first volunteer coordinator, Mrs. Eve Marris, was hired at SHW. Soon after she was hired, a series of ten volunteer orientation classes covered legal aspects, personality development, rehabilitation, and problems and principles in working with the mentally ill. Resource people included psychiatrists, psychologists and hospital managers. The psychologist, Dr. I. J. Kahan, who organized the series, became CMHA Saskatchewan executive director in 1958.

By 1957, ten employees worked in the OT Department and three in the Recreation Department. Renovations completed in 1958 created space for group and individual therapy sessions. That same year, as part of the OT and Recreation programming, a Ward Activity Department made a serious attempt to treat "hard core" patients who never left their wards. The Activity nurses tried to stimulate patients with crafts, games and music into a renewed interest in life. In 1959, the Ward Activity program expanded and its administration transferred from the OT department to nursing supervision. The nurses offered groups for gymnastics, art therapy and music therapy. Newly instigated Patient Recreation Committees gave the patients more responsibility for planning and implementing their own activities.

Volunteers and staff used music to engage and stimulate patients. An anonymous Volunteer Visitor wrote the following account called "Music and Mental Health":

*... As we enter the wards we are greeted enthusiastically by some, but many of the patients are indifferent and withdrawn. We pass out the song books to those that will accept them, and*

*begin with a well known song such as "It isn't any trouble just to S-M-I-L-E." Gradually the patients begin to relax and more singers join the group. Here is an activity requiring no special skill in which they can participate unobtrusively. For a short time at least, singing takes them out of themselves and into the charmed world of music. . Not all join in the singing. Some enjoy listening. Others keep time with hands or feet. A few will sway with the rhythm. They are given an opportunity to choose selections they would like to sing. The old familiar hymns such as "He Leadeth Me" and "What a Friend We Have in Jesus" are general favourites. Our two regular assistants from the hospital both play harmonicas and entertain with one or two rollicking numbers. Sometimes a talented singer among the patients is asked by the group leader to sing a solo. A few acting songs have been taught with good results. Special days are marked by singing songs suitable to the occasion.*

*When the time comes for us to leave the ward we find that very often the most appreciate thanks come from those who to all appearances have taken no active part in the singing. The questions, "When will you be back again?" and remarks such as "Thank You for coming. I enjoyed your playing." are very rewarding.*

Rose Schultz, one of the first music therapists at Weyburn, used music to reach people at an emotional level.[32] She described two separate interventions. For a very hyperactive woman in a manic state, Schultz put a discordant piece of music on the record player. The fast-paced composition without a regular rhythm reflected the woman's agitated state. The woman was very controlled and usually did not speak, so it was a break-through when she actually said, "Please turn that off." Schultz put on successive pieces of music, first rhythmic and fast, then slowing down to about the rhythm of the heartbeat. The woman's restlessness subsided and she left the session calmer.

Another woman was very depressed, withdrawn, with very slow movement. In this case, therapy began with slow, minor chord music and gradually increased the tempo and mood, again until the rhythm neared heart beat speed. At this point, the silent woman said, "I used to like to dance." Schultz put on an old time waltz. Since the woman had trouble walking, and to respect the physical space between them, she got a wheel chair and they danced. Soon, the woman recovered enough to return to her family.

Volunteers raised funds for the music department and introduced television to the Hospital.

*A new Hi-Fi was donated to assist with music therapy at the Hospital. Substantial donations were received from the women of Trinity Lutheran Church, The University Women's Club, and Regina Branch [of CMHA] as well as other smaller donations. In addition, records to the value of $60.00 to be used in music therapy are in the process of being purchased. The presentation of the T.V. to Dr. Humphrey Osmond, the Superintendent of the Hospital [was on T.V.]*

Staff seemed to appreciate Volunteers' feedback on the conditions and suggestions for improvements:

*Dr. Robert Sommer, research psychologist for the Hospital had a series of interviews with volunteers over quite a period of time. In a letter he says in part, "I have been very grateful for the assistance of your ladies in our interviews. This has been of considerable help to us in our attempts to design more therapeutic wards and dayrooms."*

In 1957, SHW won an International prize from the American Psychiatric Association in recognition of outstanding progress over a three-year period. The text on the silver plaque read "for outstanding accomplishment in improving the care and treatment of patients."[33]

One of the improvements at the Hospital in 1955 had been the introduction of new and more comfortable clothing for the patients. As the Hospital history noted, "Nylon dresses and socks lasted six to fifteen times longer than those made of wool."[34] In October 1958, a new project taught patients about using make-up and improved posture as well as the practice of rhythmic exercises.[35]

*Earlier in the month a Fashion Show was held at the Hospital.*

*It was planned by Mrs. E. Marris and had the assistance of Estevan, Weyburn and Regina Branches. Especially notable was the contribution made by Miss Joan Wadsworth and her models. The show itself was spectacular but it would look as though the planning period should be longer than was the case and the values involved more closely studied.*

Patients, not used to paying attention to their personal appearance, learned skills they would need when they returned to the community. Grooming was a challenge when dozens of patients used the same bathroom, and for safety's sake, no personal mirrors were allowed on the wards. Clothes, even men's boots, sent for mending, were re-issued without attention to how they fit. Finally in the 1960's, patients owned their clothing, shoes, razors, and private effects, even when they were issued by the hospital as well as when they or their families brought items for their comfort.[36]

The measures initiated to rehabilitate patients such as the stronger recreation and occupational therapy programs alleviated some of the nursing load, reduced the custodial aspect of the wards, and improved the hospital's image credibility when patients on the ward as well as those with "parole" became more active and involved.

The term "parole" reflects that in the 1950's, incarceration in the mental hospital was more legal than medical. With every door in the hospital locked, staff opened the door only after patients showed a "parole card" to go outside, to the canteen or anywhere off their own ward. Some patients with parole went downtown and often did errands for other people in the hospital. However, mailing a letter for another patient was a cause for losing parole. Staying out after curfew, misbehaviour on or off the wards, and other infractions could result in temporary or long-term loss of freedom.

After Osmond implemented an "open door" policy for some wards, controversy emerged among the citizens of Weyburn. City Council and the Chamber of Commerce expressed their concern and even alarm. Most patients used their freedom well but a few failed to return; poor social skills and boundaries brought some to the attention of the public and the R.C.M.P.[37] In those days when few people locked their homes, residents reported that the hospital inmates raided their refrigerators or gardens, and shopkeepers worried about shoplifting. People with unkempt appearance who talked loudly to unseen listeners did not have the good manners expected in public.

Not all patients caused problems. Some worked for farmers and local businesses. Patients ran a small canteen at the hospital that sold coffee, candy and other treats. Others made their own diversions. A videotaped interview on the Weyburn Hospital Virtual Museum website told about parole patients who had gardens on the hospital grounds:

*Some of them would stay out there and work all day. They would have beautiful gardens and people from town would be able to go there and purchase vegetables from them if they sold. That gave them some spending money for their tobacco or whatever they wanted... at the patients canteen.*[38]

In Kay Parley's story, some of the women canned vegetables and made jams that they stored in boxes under their beds. Parley's short story, "The Man Who Fed the Birds," told of the small shack built by one of the patients near the north gates of the Hospital. The patient watched the people coming and going from the hospital, and the birds coming and going from the nests he created from tin cans and wood. On Christmas day, and every day, this man with parole took bread crumbs and warm water to feed his birds.[39]

Other long-term patients with parole built small shelters near their garden spots where they could keep their tools and rest in the shade. Within the hospital walls there was little personal space and privacy but these people found ways to create their own space, and sought purpose and meaning in caring for their gardens (or birds).

The scope and variety of involvement of the Volunteer Visitors is evident in this annual "Report of the Volunteers to the Saskatchewan Hospital, Regina Branch, 1958":

*Once again the Volunteers of the Regina Branch had a busy and successful year, both at the Hospital and in activities in Regina. A total of 80 participated. From time to time guests from out of town accompanied the Volunteers from as far away as Ottawa. The total number of trips made was 26. The regular trip of December 31st was postponed to January 2nd and had to be cancelled because of weather conditions. During the year*

*185 relatives were carried, 22 patients, and 765 volunteers for*
*a grand total of 972. In addition a total of 20 volunteers from*
*Estevan worked with the Regina team. Average number of rel-*
*atives carried 7, patients 1, and volunteers 29-42.*

One of the highlights of every year was a fundraising tea that raised money and raised the profile of the Canadian Mental Health Association and the Volunteer program.   The wives of the provincial Premier, the Minister of Health, the Minister of Education and the Mayor of Regina poured tea. The Chair of the Volunteers reported, "The tea at the end of October was an outstanding success both from the public relations angle and from the financial one.  These funds help us materially in financing volunteer projects."

The Associated Canadian Travellers were major donors to CMHA for many years.  Volunteers served as guides for groups that visited the Hospital:

*When the Associated Canadian Travellers' motorcade went to*
*Weyburn, it was accompanied by five volunteers who assisted*
*with ushering the travellers and their friends through the Hos-*
*pital and explaining to them something about the plant, the pa-*
*tients and administration.*

In March 1959, Osmond suggested a new direction for the volunteers. In addition to the parties and activities in the hospital, visitors were asked to help with re-integrating patients into the community.  In preparation for leaving hospital, patients needed to learn about the 'outside' world and the expectations of the community around conversation, good manners and behaviour.  Major changes were new to people experiencing them for the first time: telephones, motor vehicles, and fashions. Visitors facilitated contact between patients and their families and former communities as they prepared for discharge. Osmond recognized change might be hard for the visitors, particularly for those who had established relationships with patients over the years.

In May 1959, a report to CMHA from the Volunteer Visiting Program protested the change of attitude that put restrictions on visiting at SHW:

*Since the appointment of a hospital co-ordinator of visitors, there has been a great deal of change in the visiting program. Discussions have been held with Mrs. Marris [volunteer co-ordinator], Mrs. E. Carruthers [job not identified] and Dr. H. Osmond. Limitations have been put increasingly until now the hospital asks to have every visitor named to a particular hospital ward and in some wards, every visitor to a patient. Because of distance and the total time involved it is difficult for the same visitors to come every time. Patients whom many of the visitors have known for years may only be visited after the regular visiting by going to the desk and having them brought down in the way that it is done for the ordinary visitor at the hospital. The visitors feel that the change that has come about is much too drastic and whereas a certain amount of planning by the hospital is to expected, often a great deal of visiting time has been wasted and no useful purpose accomplished.*

*There also appears to be quite a difference in thinking in the North Battleford hospital and the Weyburn one. Our visitors for instance are not allowed to see any new admissions or re-admissions. Fairly recently in the North Battleford hospital, regular parties have been arranged between the wards having new admissions and those wards that have patients ready for rehabilitation. This work is done by Saskatoon visitors.*

*Our women are pretty generally speaking the feeling that they are not wanted and consequently the attendance has suffered both in numbers and in regularity.*

After nine years at Weyburn, Osmond returned to England on September 1, 1961, sent off with a series of parties sponsored by the government, the staff and the patients of the Hospital. The new Superintendent was Dr. I. Clancy. In January 1963, Davidson received an invitation for the volunteers to learn more about the "Boarding Out Program," a foster home type of discharge for patients.

*A number of patients are out on this type of plan now and many more could probably go. The need for interested families in the*

*community and suitable homes is pressing and we wondered if
your group would be interested in hearing more about it.*

Just before Christmas in 1964, forty women braved cold stormy
weather to take Christmas treats and good wishes to four wards of geriatric patients and to the laundry at the Hospital.  Collection and distribu-
tion of Christmas gifts each year was a major project. A group of musicians went from ward to ward.  In an interview reported by the *Weyburn
Review,* Davidson commented on changes she had seen in her years of
visiting, "During the first visits, ⋯ most patients were unable to take
part in Christmas festivities; they had forgotten how.  The patient participation in both preparations and the actual party had increased a great
deal."[40]

Between 1959 and 1965, thirty volunteer visitors received 100-hour
pins (travel time not included).  By 1965, there were fewer and fewer patients in the large mental hospitals. The volunteers, like the patients,
made the transition from the institution to the community. Their attention
turned to the White Cross Centres set up by CMHA Saskatchewan to offer recreation and support for people with chronic mental illness moving
into the community.  That story continues after catching up on other de-
velopments in mental health that occurred during the era of Volunteer
Visitors.

## THE SASKATCHEWAN PLAN AND MEDICARE

When CMHA Saskatchewan was founded in 1950, the Cooperative Commonwealth Federation (CCF, forerunner of the New Democratic Party) had been in office under Premier T.C. Douglas since June 1944. Douglas represented Weyburn, and had a strong interest in issues of health care including mental illness and treatment.

Dr. Henry Sigerist of Johns Hopkins University had advised the Department of Public Health in September 1944 on a whole range of health care including "regional homes for the elderly, care of mental defectives, treatment of the mentally ill, and the establishment of a medical school." The Sigerist Commission proposed a long-term goal of "a government-operated hospital insurance plan for the whole province." [41] The next year, Hincks made similar recommendations.

The CCF caucus met regularly with socially conscious groups. The CMHA Saskatchewan archives documented an established pattern of annual briefs to the government, drawing attention to the significant needs for reform but also applauding the intentions and actions of the Department of Public Health. The government took such opportunities to remind the public of the gains in mental health care. For example, in 1945, the "free-care" policy increased hospital funding so that families of patients in mental hospitals were not charged room and board.[42] In 1950, a new provincial *Mental Health Act* changed the purpose of mental hospitals from "custody to therapy."[43] Outpatient community clinics, full-time in Regina and Saskatoon and part-time in North Battleford, Weyburn and Moose Jaw, provided consultation to family doctors as well as public education.[44]

Starting in 1952, the CMHA promoted what came to be called *The Saskatchewan Plan* in their annual briefs. The Saskatchewan Plan advocated good medical and counseling services close to where people lived and worked, for early intervention in emotional and psychiatric difficulties. The Plan recommended rehabilitation to help released patients back to a more normal life in the community as a way to reduce the likelihood of readmission. The original plan also specified reducing the size of the two large mental hospitals and building eight regional mental hospitals, each with about 150 beds. The smaller hospitals, closer to people's homes would enable the mentally ill to receive treatment equivalent to care for the physically ill.[45]

In 1955, McKerracher left government to become Head of the Psychiatry Department at the new College of Medicine at the University of Saskatchewan in Saskatoon. Dr. Sam Lawson, the new director of PSB advocated the Saskatchewan Plan through his roles with the government and with the CMHA Scientific Advisory Committee.[46] A 1956 CMHA Saskatchewan annual meeting resolution demanded that provincial government implement the Saskatchewan Plan system of regional hospitals. To strengthen its position, CMHA had garnered support from the Saskatoon District Medical Society, the Saskatoon Board of Trade, the Saskatoon Community Chest, Saskatchewan United Farm Women and the Saskatchewan Homemakers' Clubs. The Cabinet deemed the cost of eight new facilities prohibitive.[47]

CMHA made its call for regional hospitals more public. A *Regina Leader-Post* article of March 15, 1957 titled, "Mental health aid criticized" provoked a letter from Premier T. C. Douglas that challenged the CMHA endorsement and pressure for eight new hospitals. Mrs. N. M. Toombs, provincial president, responded that CMHA must continually bring forward the issue that mental health care should be comparable to physical care.[48]

In April, correspondence between Toombs and Mr. George Rohn, Executive Director of CMHA Saskatchewan, planned editorials and letters to the Regina, Saskatoon and weekly papers. Toombs expressed frustration at the investment in the two old hospitals and their growing population as out-moded places where people were put away. Toombs' handwritten note concluded:

> *The $300,000 that is being spent on the roof at Weyburn is no doubt needed but this is not helping to provide better treatment for the mentally ill, and the $100,000 to be spent on the one addition at Battleford is not providing treatment; it is simply*

*housing elderly patients, giving them custodial care until they die.*

*Please don't put anything like this in the paper or I'll get another letter from Mr. Douglas. Remember the Rod and the Carrot.*[49]

Indeed letters to the editors published in newspapers in Regina, Saskatoon, Prince Albert and some community papers criticized the budget estimates in the spring of 1957 and closed with a warning:

*We want to sincerely assure the Government that our 30,000 members[c] in Saskatchewan, together with a number of province-wide organizations, are prepared to do their share once the Government demonstrates its determination to solve the problem. ... Our members and friends are however, just as ready to express their dissatisfaction. ... Will the Government provide the leadership?*[50]

In preparation for the fall presentation of the brief to government, Lewis A. Henbury from the Division office cautioned Osmond in a confidential letter:

*Although there are still many things we feel the Government should do for the Mentally Ill, I feel it is in the best interests of all concerned, if in making a strong plan for even greater improvements, we temper our requests with a few gracious remarks about improvements which have already been effected."*[51]

Prior to 1957, the CMHA briefs to government tended to praise the government for its innovation and commitment to mental health. The 1957 brief included detailed criticism and again demanded the construction of eight new hospitals. When the brief was presented, the provincial government announced that instead of new hospitals, psychiatric wards

---

[c]   The 1956 Census of Saskatchewan showed a total population of 880,665 persons.   http://www.statcan.gc.ca/pub/11-516-x/sectiona/A2_14-eng.csv  accessed March 30, 2012.

would be integrated into general hospitals. McKerracher had proposed this alternative to put physical and psychiatric care on a more even footing. He argued that local psychiatric services with time-limited hospital stays prepared patients for return to their family, home and community.

At this same time, the provincial government was negotiating with the federal government for cost-shared hospital insurance. Douglas wrote to CMHA explaining that the federal *Hospital Insurance and Diagnostic Services Act* covered acute illness, but not long-term chronic care in mental hospitals and nursing homes.[52]   Neither Lawson nor the CMHA Board appeared to recognize and accept the financial and political implications.[53]

An experiment in the Swift Current health region from 1958 to 1960 demonstrated that community services actually reduced the number of people sent to the Weyburn Hospital. A psychiatrist, Dr. Frederic Grunberg, and a psychiatric social worker Miss Beverly Pruden, conducted outpatient clinics in Swift Current, Shaunavon, Maple Creek and Leader.[54] Swift Current municipal taxes covered the costs of doctors, hospitalization and drugs through a medical insurance plan that served as a forerunner of Medicare.

The 1959-60 election campaign introduced Douglas' dream for universal medical care insurance.   Despite government promises for the

*Keep Our Doctors Demonstration 1962*
*Saskatchewan Archives Board RA-12,109*

construction of a psychiatric centre in Yorkton, CMHA distrusted the CCF's commitment to the Saskatchewan Plan.[55] CMHA supported the College of Physicians and Surgeons and the business communities in opposing Medicare. The CMHA Scientific Planning Committee, under the leadership of Hoffer, conducted a letterwriting campaign to ask the provincial government to build the regional centres before the expense of Medicare made the new construction impossible.[56]

On August 4, 1961 Douglas left his position as premier to take on the leadership of the federal New Democratic Party (NDP). The new premier, Woodrow Lloyd, announced that the work on the Yorkton Centre would resume, and promised a psychiatric research centre in Saskatoon, a long-held dream of Hoffer. Nevertheless, CMHA continued to oppose Medicare and supported the College of Physicians and Surgeons in their 23-day doctors' strike in July 1962.[57]

The Yorkton Psychiatric Centre opened on September 30, 1964 with 120 beds. Its design was a modified form of the architecture proposed by Izumi as a result of the Weyburn LSD experiments. The Yorkton Centre also adopted the Saskatchewan Plan philosophy of outpatient clinics, shorter hospital stays and a team approach to treating people in their own homes, and found they required fewer beds.[58]

In the 1960's, as CMHA championed the idea of separate psychiatric facilities, it changed its relationship with government. Lawson retired from PSB in 1965. Today, CMHA advocates full citizenship and mental health care with appropriate and adequate resources in the community. Through the models of empowerment and recovery, the goal is for people to live the fullest lives possible in the least restrictive environments. The Saskatchewan Plan is now remembered positively as a movement to disburse mental health services closer to the communities where people live. Medicare changed the delivery of mental health services.

The history of mental health under Medicare continues after the next chapter about the White Cross Centres, another illustration of the transition from institutional to community care.

# THE ROAD BACK FROM MENTAL ILLNESS IS EASIER TODAY!

When a patient leaves the mental hospital, his battle may be only half over. Having conquered his mental illness, he may now have to overcome other obstacles—prejudice, friendlessness, lack of follow-up medical care.

Fortunately, the returning mental patient is no longer on his own. Today his mental health association is by his side to help him find a job, new friends, and additional psychiatric care if needed.

Meanwhile, the association is supporting new research, seeking new and better ways to treat mental illness, even to prevent it. Help keep these vital programs going. Join and support your mental health association!

*The Road Back from Mental Illness Publicity Photo 1962*
*Saskatchewan Archives Board RB-12,262*

## WHITE CROSS CENTRE BEGINNINGS

The government pushed the idea of people with mental illness leaving the large mental hospitals and living in their own homes. The hospital tried to prepare patients through OT, group programs, and short visits out of hospital. People who had lived for years in hospital routine had not made decisions about their lives, not even what to cook for supper. They re-entered society with minimal plans for their continuing care and comfort in the community. For some patients, after years of close association with other patients and staff, discharge felt like abandonment and isolation. Despite its drawbacks, a mental hospital offered a range of necessities for patients: housing, meals, recreation, health care, and occupational therapy through crafts or necessary work. Although the government Health department was saving money with fewer patients in hospital, those funds were not being channeled into community services to meet the needs of ex-patients and people with chronic mental illness. The total control of a person's life in the hospital "institutionalized" them so that they were unprepared for the stress of small and large decisions. Lawson said about older chronic patients:

> ... *For to grow old in hospital means literally to lose your identity. You soon have no one to belong to and no one belonging to you ... while family and friends, goals like happiness, good life and success, become correspondingly less important.*[59]

Some people readjusted with the help of family and neighbours. They got jobs, reunited with their families or made new friends, and took up their citizenship. Some patients returned to families who were unprepared, and unsupported, to care for them. Senior citizens went to nursing homes nearer to their families. Approved Homes and group homes opened with landladies who provided board and room paid through welfare.  Released patients who could not cope became caught in the revolving door of hospital admissions and discharges.

People had lost the skills necessary to care for themselves and essential tasks such as cooking were unfamiliar:

> *In a female geriatric ward it was found that patients averaged 21 years since last cooking a full meal, 11 since boiling an egg, 19 since baking a cake and 16 since making soup.  Many had never seen an electric stove or mixer before.  Less than a third wanted to cook; they said they wouldn't know how or that they were satisfied with the present hospital foods.*[60]

After the constant interactions and activities of the hospital, people's days felt even longer without work or outside interests.  CMHA advocated for more rehabilitation services to offer vocational, social, recreation, therapeutic and general support for patients leaving hospital and for people newly diagnosed in the community.   In the mid-1950s, CMHA developed a pilot project for rehabilitation services.   Since this was a pilot project, the job description specified that the worker planned the services and researched established programs and "obstacles that hinder the patient's rehabilitation." The definition of rehabilitation specified

> *the restoration of the patient to the fullest physical, mental, social, vocational and economic usefulness of which he [or she] is capable. Rehabilitation is only complete when the person is enabled to live as full and satisfying a family life and as full and satisfying a work life as is possible for him [or her] in view of his [or her] handicap.*

To focus on restoring the person to the most "full and satisfying life" the social worker assessed the needs and problems of the person's health, social and life circumstances, as well as emotional or personality problems.

> *The social worker would interview the patient to determine the patient's motivation, interpret the illness to family, employer and others directly concerned.  The social worker would help the patient make use of available treatment and vocational*

*adjustment along with personal and social adjustment. The patient should do as much as he [or she] is capable of.*[61]

With the ultimate goal of mainstream employment for people returning to the community, the social worker also evaluated job skills. The job description recognized the difficulty of placing long time patients with chronic mental illness: "Vocational help and job finding were necessary, but one of the more difficult functions." Often the person had not developed the skills and habits necessary for employment. Employers were reluctant to take a risk on someone for whom occupational programs in hospital were their previous work experience.

The social worker acted as a liaison with the hospital, and hospital psychiatrists, during the discharge process, received discharge information and assisted in follow-up. The worker was expected to know the community resources including the Department of Welfare, and to foster relationships with potential employers. The first White Cross Centre was designed as a one-stop resource for released patients.

An early history described the beginnings of the White Cross Centre in Regina:

> ... *the first rehabilitation center in Saskatchewan opened in November 1955 at 1755 Scarth Street with A. S. Mayotte as its first rehabilitation director, for patients and ex-patients from mental hospitals. It had a large room where they could dance to records. There were shelves full of games for their use. It had a small kitchenette where coffee and sandwiches could be made and another room for table tennis. It had offices for staff.*[62]

Volunteer Visitors with the White Cross Centres continued to entertain patients in their homes or at the Centre, and encouraged groups of people living in group homes to get together for fun and conversation in the evenings. The Centres operated by CMHA in Regina and Weyburn offered programs for patients released from the large mental hospitals as well as new patients from the Munroe Wing at the Regina General and Grey Nuns (now Pasqua) Hospitals. At first, volunteers staffed the Centres but soon professional personnel, social workers and psychologists, directed the programs.

The CMHA 1957 Brief to government that had advocated the Saskatchewan Plan pointed out that rehabilitation was one of the most neglected areas of community mental health work in Saskatchewan. CMHA Saskatchewan President Toombs and Executive Director George Rohn described the Association's role in rehabilitation programs as experimental, a pilot project with the expectation that government would take on the task once its value had been proved. They noted that in its first year of operation, the Rehabilitation Centre had benefited ex-patients and relatives as well as the hospital in Weyburn. As part of the plan to bring hospitals and rehabilitation programs to centers closer to peoples' homes, CMHA expected that the PSB would employ more social workers for community services in Regina and other areas of the province. CMHA asserted that expanding the White Cross Centre services would be "too large a task for a voluntary organization."

*We commend the Government for appointing a consultant in the field of rehabilitation and we sincerely hope that expansion of the program will take place in the near future. It might be well to explore ways and means for the use of the Federal Rehabilitation grants in the rehabilitation for the mentally ill.*[63]

Mental health services operated on two diverging tracks, beginning work in the community while maintaining the large hospitals. The CMHA Saskatchewan Newsletter #1 in 1958 reflected this complexity as they celebrated community rehabilitation centres but also donated equipment to the SHNB. They reported the opening of the Swift Current Rehabilitation Centre. Saskatoon had expanded to a full-time Social Worker for the White Cross Centre, as more patients from North Battleford needed help to get a job and a place to live. On the other track, CMHA purchased a piano for the large OT room in North Battleford where the patients had formed a small orchestra.[64]

Saskatchewan was proud of its reputation for leading the way from deinstitutionalization to rehabilitation. However, most of the provincial government's budget remained tied up in the large institutions. The Saskatchewan Plan with its emphasis on local psychiatric facilities and community services was never truly implemented. The need for community-based services became more obvious. Preparing people for discharge formed an important part of the early White Cross programs. CMHA also struggled to make the public aware of and responsive to the needs of the ex-patients returning to their communities. CMHA Saskatchewan prepared stories for city and rural newspapers, "Coming home is worse for these people than coming as a stranger. They have all the wrong information, because their memories have remained stagnant while changes went on apace."[65]

CMHA news releases, pamphlets and public meetings informed and educated the public who expressed apprehension as so many ex-patients were returned to their communities. Kahan, CMHA Saskatchewan executive director wrote of the apprehensions that patients experienced:

> *"[Henry] had been taken to the mental hospital by horse and buggy, and was returning in a new-model car." His friend Bob helps re-orient to noisy streets, the supermarket and the barber shop.*

> *...Patients like Henry, who had been in hospital as long as 20 years, comprise 40% of the over-60 age group in mental hospitals. Because mental illness does not kill, because present treatments are ineffective on chronic patients and hospitals inadequate, this group has increased, creating new problems in psychiatric and physical care, hospital maintenance and old age.[66]*

Kahan emphasized the importance of the White Cross Centres as part of integrating patients into the community and relearning skills for daily living. Deinstitutionalization in Saskatchewan was a large-scale experiment from which other provinces and countries benefited in the long run. As it unfolded, CMHA evaluated what worked and what didn't. Kahan asked, "Why do some of these discharges succeed while others fail? It is not known why, or how helpful it would be to send such a patient home for short visits before discharge."[67]

White Cross Centres provided a place where people with mental illness would be accepted and supported. A handout "to be used by interested lay people who are active workers of CMHA" documented this desire:

> *Most ex-patients felt that they needed help in building their confidence and feeling of personal dignity and security, and that the biggest barrier to recovery was their own sense of in-*

*adequacy and insecurity. It was found further that ex-patients valued the friendship of other ex-patients and patients.*

*...At first, membership was small. But not for long. Ex-patients found that they could come and be themselves "without people looking at me as though I had two heads." They could be with others who had problems similar to theirs.*

*They could, perhaps, get help in planning a monthly budget or finding a place to live. If they wished solitude, they could come and sit alone in the recreation room, knowing no questions would be asked or eyebrows raised. Here you could bring your fears, your anger, your need for a friend. Here, too, friendships were made, romances begun. Club members could rejoice, disagree and sympathize with one another, without someone standing in judgment of their behaviour.[68]*

People accustomed to a structured environment needed to learn to enjoy leisure with time for activities and time for personal reflection. [69] Acceptance, safety and "peer support" were important to people learning to live with mental illness in the community. Patients looked out for one another. They monitored each other for signs of illness that might indicate a need for more help. When a member returned from another hospital stay, the members welcomed the person back, "The more relaxed members drew the more timid ones into games, making sure that no one sat through an evening unnoticed. They felt that no one else understood them as well as themselves."[70]

Not only patients but also their families looked to the CMHA White Cross Centres for assistance and advice:

*Often families phone and say, "My son or daughter has nowhere to go, can she come to your club?" ... Just as often, [parents] phone to say, "My son (or daughter) is easier to get along with since coming to the club."*

*From its primary function of providing a safe and accepting place for patients and ex-patients, the Centre has become a place where one faces many of one's problems. It is also a place where one can get advice. A husband may come in to say that the wife seems ill and incapable of looking after the children. What to do, whom to see? What if she doesn't cooperate? A friend does nothing but sit in his room all day. How to help him? Patients, employers, wives, husbands, friends ... phone from all parts of the province.*

As White Cross Centres opened in other communities, CMHA Saskatchewan appointed a Rehabilitation Committee for the development and oversight of the programs. The Committee met regularly to discuss policy, procedures and solve problems. They also advocated with PSB for improved services such as a Mental Health Clinic in Prince Albert and an increase in boarding-out rates for patients who were placed in private homes, designated as Approved Homes.[71]

The Saskatoon White Cross Centre, with ties to SHNB, also reached out to the psychiatric ward at University Hospital, contacting psychiatrists for referrals.[72] Popularly known as the Victory Club, the Saskatoon rehabilitation programs offered arts and crafts, games night, afternoon bridge, and Friday evening films or dancing. For variety they added bowling, summer outings, drives around the city and frequent visits to homes of White Cross Centre volunteers and members. Parties for birthdays and holidays developed skills for planning and organizing along with having fun and staying in touch with the changing seasons.[73]

Paying for the White Cross Centre programming was already an issue. The 1960 CMHA annual meeting discussed the respective roles of government and CMHA in provision and funding of the rehabilitation services. CMHA expected that PSB would take over the rehabilitation programs. Gradually, CMHA realized that if they continued to run the programs, they needed annual grants. Division board requested a $10,000 rehabilitation grant from the Saskatchewan Government.

This program funding moved White Cross Centres from pilot projects to CMHA programs, from an innovative experiment for services which government would eventually provide, to direct services through the voluntary, non-profit organization. The Scientific Planning Committee developed a Divisional policy regarding function, membership, evaluation study, and roles of White Cross Centre Committees, supervisors, White Cross Centre Directors and Group Leaders.[74]

After Miss B. Jaksa, the first White Cross Centre Director resigned, the job description reflected the change of emphasis from pilot project to CMHA program.  The voluntary organization could not sustain the full range of services that helped people find housing and jobs, provided education and support to Approved Home operators and other tasks that proved the need for such services. By 1960 the White Cross Centres concentrated on the social programs.

> *The function of our White Cross Centre is to promote social rehabilitation.  In effect, our centres are established as community clubs for former patients.  Social activity programs are set up to enable the club members to learn to participate socially, to help them form good relationships, and to give them a feeling of acceptance and personal worth.*[75]

The Director staffed the Regina White Cross Centre, managed the clubs in Saskatoon, Swift Current and Weyburn and was expected to expand the program to North Battleford and Prince Albert.  The complex duties included administration, policy development, guidance and leadership for volunteers. Liaison with mental hospitals, various professionals, and clubs and organizations opened opportunities to ask for their help with the programs.  Public education in social rehabilitation, needs of former patients and the mentally ill, and the philosophies and aims of the Canadian Mental Health Association involved speaking to community organizations and writing reports for newspapers and periodicals.[76]

The new Director, Miss Joyce Harman reported increased activities, volunteers and member attendance in all the White Cross Centres.  The Rotary Club in Regina offered financial, transportation and other assistance and sent a member to the Committee.  The White Cross Centre in Regina hosted a field program for student nurses to further the role of the nurse in social rehabilitation.  In 1960, the Kinsmen Club of Swift Current provided transportation to bring members to the White Cross Centre and to the Saturday Club for retarded children.  Community organizations mobilized to open the White Cross Centre in North Battleford.  As the programs expanded, the supervisors in the various cities requested increases in their honoraria.[77]  Staffing and funding the White Cross Centres became a major issue for CMHA.

Requests for funding from the growing number of community-based organizations became an issue for the Saskatchewan government. It established the Office of the Provincial Coordinator on Rehabilitation to deal with the increasing demands. The polio epidemic had brought more public awareness of the needs of children and adults with handicaps. At least five different organizations[78] operated rehabilitation programs and applied to the government for funding. The federal and provincial budgets allocated funds directly to programs like the Department of Rehabilitation Medicine at University Hospital in Saskatoon. The Department of Social Welfare was responsible for assessment, counseling and training of people with handicaps. People affected by polio, and paraplegic patients, needed medical care and rehabilitation. The government was also responsible for the Bureau on Alcoholism. The Department of Education paid for special education classes and schools. The Department of Health covered treatment in hospitals including psychiatric treatment or follow up by public health, doctors and psychiatrists. Social welfare payments for persons with disabilities were not accounted as rehabilitation expenses. In each of these non-government and government services, the biggest cost was staff salaries while the lack of qualified staff posed a critical problem.[79]

The Co-ordination Council on Rehabilitation Saskatchewan consulted 63 government and non-government organizations and prepared a report for the Advisory Committee on Medical Care.[80] The new definition of rehabilitation mentioned the necessities for living as well as "judicious" use of professional skills and community resources needed to cope with disability:

> *Ideally, it can be argued that for any disability, injury, or illness that occurs, restoration of every person towards optimum function is desirable. The rehabilitation process cannot, therefore, be divorced from the regular health, welfare, and education services of the community ... For practical purposes, it becomes necessary to consider the rehabilitation process ...more narrowly..., recognizing such realistic limits as finances, facilities, personnel supply, public demand and potential recovery of the individual in relation to the effort expended.*

In other words, the public, and organizations representing persons with disabilities, could not expect unlimited resources to meet their needs. Instead of the earlier ideal of "optimum function" or what CMHA had called "a full and satisfying life", the new standard was more modest, "a functional goal would seem to be the restoration of handicapped persons to a level adequate for them to maintain their place in society with minimal dependence on others."[81]

Government assumed that the basic services were already in place for all persons in society, and argued that persons with "special" needs already benefited from the social, education and health services of the province. The Provincial Coordinator on Rehabilitation of Disabled Persons estimated that the community-based organizations contributed voluntary funds and programs worth approximately one-third of the $1.5 million dollars spent annually on "special services to the handicapped."

Recommendations in the *Special Report on Rehabilitation of Handicapped Persons in Saskatchewan* called for the comprehensive planning and coordination of rehabilitation services through government departments of health, education and welfare. The report encouraged further development of the Coordinating Council of 35 non-government rehabilitation organizations and the relevant government departments. [82]

The *Special Report* described, "The Canadian Mental Health Association provides recreation and social adjustment programs and a limited support of classes for the mentally retarded."[83] Under gaps in physical and mental health services, the brief listed "guidance and support to post-psychotic cases, necessary for adjustment into the community, are almost non-existent."[84]

> *A complete range of services is, in a sense, a minimum requirement. For instance, the benefits of existing medical and psychiatric restorative services are diminished or dissipated without the complementary support (psychological, social, educational and vocational) required by the disabled to achieve maximum independence. Successful treatment of persons suffering from psychosis, for example, is of questionable value without sufficient skilled social and vocational staff to rehabilitate the patient into the community.*[85]

Doctors, hospitals, medications and mental health clinics limited their services to the medical needs of persons with chronic and acute mental illness. As a voluntary agency without adequate funding, CMHA could not meet the high psychological, social, educational and vocational needs of people living with mental illness. The new population of persons who received counseling and treatment for mental disorders might never have been hospitalized but that did not mean that their illnesses were less severe and disabling. In 1961, the Weyburn White Cross Centre was encouraged to move beyond programs for inpatients and ex-patients to people from the community with emotional problems referred by ministers and general practitioners. That policy change was accepted by the Division Board and implemented in other White Cross Centres.[86]

North Battleford rented the Empress Theatre for the White Cross Centre and hired the Supervisor at $90 per month for keeping the Centre open three days a week.[87] The gap between the community organization wages and the government wages was evident because a government Psychiatric Services Worker position was advertised at $312 to $379 per month.[88]

Members clubs, self-help groups and staff-run programming emerged in various communities across North America as more people were released from hospitals into the community. CMHA Saskatchewan contributed to, and learned from, those initiatives. Fountain House, begun in New York in 1957, operated as a community within the community and created a "restorative environment for individuals who had been socially and vocationally disabled by mental illness. "Fountain House is a membership club and individuals are members, not patients or clients, to promote a sense of belonging."[89] It did not operate as a drop-in. Instead, attendance was expected and members greeted one another each day to create a welcoming environment. Instead of staff-directed programs, Fountain House participants, both members and paid leaders, worked together to make the program work. For example, in the pre-vocational day program, if the floor needed to be washed, staff and members took on that task together, not as teacher and learner or manager and assistant, but as a team doing what needed to be done. The "human desire to be needed" was the most important motivator.

The Fountain House model addressed employment, socialization, and housing. Even the most disabled persons worked because productive work was "essential to increase confidence and the potential for future gainful employment." Fountain House contracted with regular employers, businesses and agencies and the workers received "regular wages in unsubsidized jobs." In-house opportunities for work included the thrift shop, clubhouse newsletters, and operation and maintenance of the clubhouse. In the Transitional Employment Program, the employer hired Fountain House who ensured that a member, or if necessary a staff person, completed the job without adjustment or lowering of work standards and without any subsidy to employers. Staff and members worked together as equals – two or more people with the goal of doing the job well.

The Fountain House model believed "that men and women require opportunities to be together socially." The clubhouse offered a place for conversation, relaxation, and social support every evening, weekends and especially, holidays. This recognized that for people who are not closely connected to families and neighbours, "time off" could be especially lonely and disheartening. Through the "reach out" program, members and staff sought out persons who had not attended the programs, found out why, and if suitable, brought them back into regular contact.

In addition to the vocational and social programming, Fountain House apartments offered adequate, pleasant and affordable housing. Members also had access to medication, psychiatric and physical health care; New York did not have Medicare. Everyone, regardless of disability, participated in decision-making, evaluation and clubhouse accountability.

The Fountain House Model influenced the direction of White Cross Centres, and representatives of Fountain House visited Saskatchewan to see the Centres in 1960. Kahan publicized their interest:

> *The Regina Centre, the first and oldest, has attracted attention from many agencies throughout the continent, including Fountain House Foundation, Inc., New York. It has been estimated that the readmission rate of Regina club members to mental hospital is less than one third of that of the general Regina population, an encouraging figure. "Our club members," says I. J. Kahan, executive director of the Saskatchewan CMHA, "stay better longer."*[90]

The White Cross Centres struggled to define their role and identity. The Divisional Rehabilitation Committee balanced normalization expecting members to be responsible with minimizing risk and ensuring appropriate support. For example, the August 1961 minutes record:

*There was a discussion on whether or not breakable articles should be placed in the club rooms for use by the members. It was decided that it is our duty to teach the club members in this respect, however, it is important that we should not be too critical.*

*The question was raised ... of what should be done in case of emergencies regarding patients. This is in regard to such places as Saskatoon where the Supervisor is not available at all times and the social workers are out of town. Mrs. Miller stated that a list of the members' doctors would be very helpful. It was suggested that such a list could be left at the disposal of the personnel concerned. It was recommended that Miss Harman investigate the matter further.[91]*

Committee members noted that people who came into the White Cross Centre programs tended to remain members and continued to use the services. The White Cross Centres thought of themselves as a transition service between hospital and community. They anticipated that after that transition, members would no longer require the club. The question was raised, "if not enough of our club members are graduating, then possibly there is something wrong with our program."[92]

The Committee debated whether the production of goods and services or the social recreational activities were most important for the clients and the Centres.[93] In the early days, organizers expected ex-patients to get jobs and attend the White Cross Centre for recreation during evenings and weekends. When it became obvious that some patients were not ready for regular employment, the White Cross Centre took on contracts to assemble, sort or make items. Into the 1970s, former patients took apart telephones, power meters and other equipment for recycling. A crew assembled plastic bags with a fork, napkin, and condiments for a fast food chain. A participant remembers turning countless strips of coloured plastic into "flowers" used to decorate parade floats and wedding cars. Members stuffed envelopes or shredded documents for CMHA and businesses that contracted for this service. Workers were paid a small honorarium, a few dollars a month, to ensure that their "earned income" was under the maximum allowed for people on Income Assistance. Being part of a group with social stops for tea and conversation, plus a sense of purpose and a reason to get up every day, assisted re-entry into community participation, even if it did not lead to long-term paid employment.

By the end of the 1980's, William A. Anthony, a professor in rehabilitation services from Boston, U.S.A., proclaimed the end of the era of deinstitutionalization and the launch of the era of rehabilitation. He cited Fountain House as an example and commended self-help groups springing up in both Canada and the United States under the leadership of consumers. Anthony wrote:

> *Deinstitutionalization focused on how buildings function; rehabilitation focuses on how people function. Deinstitutionalization focused on closing buildings; rehabilitation focuses on opening lives. Deinstitutionalization focused on getting rid of patient restraints; rehabilitation focuses on getting hold of person supports.[94]*

In Saskatchewan, both the government and the CMHA expressed pride in their reputation as a world leader for closing large mental hospitals, and for demanding and providing community support for people living in the community with mental illness.

# GOVERNMENT SERVICES AND CMHA IN THE 1960'S

The Departments of Health, Education and Social Services faced major changes in mental health delivery during the 1960s. The Saskatchewan *Mental Health Act* of 1961 changed hospital admission to a doctor's decision instead of a judicial order. People with mental illness were deemed to be ill rather than dangerous. This was reflected in a language change so that patients were released from hospital rather than paroled. In-patient parole was renamed off-ward privileges or day passes. CMHA continued to educate the public that mental diagnoses were illnesses to be treated, not feared. The movement to community-based mental health continued under the Liberal government led by Ross Thatcher elected in 1964.

The introduction of Medicare had changed the delivery of mental health services. A number of psychiatrists and other professionals left the province, partly because the smaller patient load at the mental hospitals reduced the number employed in Weyburn and North Battleford. Remaining psychiatrists worked in mental health clinics or established private practices. Medicare paid for patient visits and hospital stays but the private psychiatrists, no longer on salary, conferred about fee-for-service rates for consultations to family physicians and community mental health clinics. The psychiatrist's fee schedule had no category for supporting family members or community agencies.

Full-time mental health clinics were established in larger centers with psychiatrists and mental health workers traveling to other communities, such as Melfort, Lloydminster and Kindersley. Psychiatric nurses and social workers provided counseling and monitored medication effects through regular appointments at the clinic or in the patient's home.

Psychiatric wards, already in Regina and Saskatoon , were added to hospitals in Prince Albert, Moose Jaw, and Swift Current.   The Saskatchewan Hospitals at Weyburn and North Battleford continued to serve local and provincial needs. The Yorkton Mental Health Centre, the only new facility built under the original Saskatchewan Plan, opened in 1964.

*Yorkton Psychiatric Centre Main Entrance 1964*
*Saskatchewan Archives Board PS-64-048-03*

Family physicians and local hospitals assumed more responsibility for community mental health services through outpatient care and admissions to psychiatric beds in community hospitals. In 1964, Dr. Colin M. Smith, Director of PSB, attended a conference sponsored by the Canadian Medical Association, the Canadian Psychiatric Association and CMHA National. *Medical Action for Mental Health* continued to debate the need for separate psychiatric facilities, but also recognized the provision of psychiatric services by family doctors. Psychiatrists asked to be considered equal to other specialists in medicine.  McKerracher chaired the panel on Community Psychiatry, championing the value of the General Practitioner caring for people "with chronic neurosis and lifelong difficulties" providing they had access to good consultation services." [95]

The Canada Assistance Plan of 1966 coordinated income support under an agreement between the federal and provincial governments. Welfare distributed through the Department of Social Services ensured regular, although minimal, income for discharged patients in the community and for people living with disability and unemployment.  Income support covered operators of Approved Homes for room and board for their residents.  Income assistance supplied an essential ingredient in the shift from institutional to community-based living.

The professionals looked forward to a day when even long-term patients were released into the community.  Early tranquilizers and antipsychotic medications treated symptoms of anxiety and disturbed thinking. Electro-convulsive treatments (ECT) reduced depression and delusions.  The new remedies also brought debilitating side effects but they made the patient easier to manage, less violent, and more compliant. The Admissions Wards at Saskatchewan Hospitals concentrated on more intensive therapy to return patients to their homes. One man, who was released after months in the mental hospital, shared his story for the Regina Leader-Post in January 1960.[96]

> *Regular electric shock treatments are held at the hospital on doctor's orders. You lie on a bed and are put under an anesthetic before treatment.*

> *I began to get better with these treatments. My doctor assured me that my political and religious beliefs were no business of the hospital's, and I felt new freedom and individuality, as I began to stand on my own feet again.*

> *Those snooker, cribbage and rummy games took on a greater lure, and I began to enjoy table tennis. I hadn't played baseball before I went into hospital. Now I was scoring home runs. ... Now I could enjoy the gymnastic exercises, bowling, dances, films and the wiener-roasts on the grounds.*

Both the formal system and CMHA were heartened by advances in medicine and improved quality of life for people. The PSB, later called the Mental Health Services Branch, was part of the Department of Health. CMHA was a voluntary, non-government organization. They were two separate entities that worked together when it suited their purposes. Sometimes they found themselves on opposite sides of a decision, or at least so it appeared. The government needed CMHA to create a public will, and community acceptance, for the movement of patients from hospitals into their communities. CMHA valued the professionals who also volunteered with the Association. By the mid-1960s, the government figured out that CMHA White Cross Centres delivered services more economically than programs delivered by higher paid government employees. But one purpose of CMHA was to hold government accountable for providing adequate mental health programs and services. Dependence on government grants made CMHA more vulnerable.

The Scientific Planning Committee discussed a "conflict in interests, or a conflict in loyalties" in April 1966. Most members were government employees *and* members of a Committee answerable through CMHA to the public. They agreed the Committee, not individual members, advised the Board; thus members were under no obligation to follow the advice of the CMHA Board on the practice of their given professions. Professionals found it helpful to suggest improvements for service in the safety of a committee so that CMHA, not the government employee, criticized the inadequacy and advocated for change. A suggestion to change the name to Professional Advisory Committee (PAC) noted "that while such a name may not carry as much status, it probably was a more accurate description of the role that the Committee played."[97] By 1968, the office file name changed to "Advisory -- Scientific Planning Committee."[98] Subgroups of the Scientific Planning Committee worked with some of the branches. Professionals on the CMHA Saskatoon Advisory Committee recommended closer links between the PSB and CMHA to "improve research methods and their application in the service of the public."

In January 1968, a Special Advisory Committee of CMHA Saskatoon met "to formulate a statement regarding the research field." For several years, Hoffer had been receiving grants for the Malvaria project to investigate the role of niacin and vitamin C in the treatment of schizophrenia. The committee noted the needs for pure research and postgraduate studies. Members of the committee drew attention to the public interest in problems of emotionally disturbed children, and the relationship of these childhood disturbances to home life, school programs, and mental and social stability, including the cost to the community.

The Saskatoon committee developed a proposal to phase in research for emotionally disturbed children so that CMHA could "advise the Saskatchewan Government on the needs of these children five years hence, on the basis of knowledge locally gained."[99] Pilot projects included the full range of services from facilities for pre-school children to teens, in their own homes or in residential treatment alternatives. Children continued in ordinary schools, or if necessary received education in the residence or hospital. Plans included a research control population for matched studies with children not assisted during the five-year period. Stephen from the MacNeill Clinic noted that the $200 grant from CMHA was not sufficient to begin to examine 300 pre-school children for physical and mental health instability.

The White Cross Centre in Saskatoon had also asked for the Advisory Committee's advice. The Committee recommended that the White Cross Centre move from the Mental Health Clinic building. A policy of enforcing attendance would have required bigger premises, adequate staffing and the equipment for a sheltered workshop with social and recreational activities during non-working hours.

The Saskatoon committee summarized:

*Our views have covered the fields of better facilities for our patients; research, pure and applied; and professional education. We foresee the ultimate purpose of CMHA as an informed group working in harmony with the Provincial Health Department. In later days, it should be able to advise the Government of Saskatchewan on planning better and relatively less expensive mental health services on a basis of real, local knowledge and adequate surveys of needs carefully elaborated by panels of experts covering a wide field of relevant professional disciplines.*[100]

In February 1968, CMHA executive director Kahan wrote a long memo to Hoffer, chair of the Advisory-Scientific Planning Committee

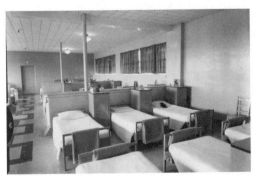

*Dormitory in Saskatchewan Training School Cottage Moose Jaw, 1957*
*Saskatchewan Archives Board PS-57-749-10*

about setting priorities for the Saskatchewan Division programs. He discussed several issues including the CMHA role for children with mental retardation, policies for research, and the feasibility of asking the government to fund the White Cross Centre programs.

When it was founded, CMHA acted as an advocate for children with mental illness and people with mental retardation housed in the mental hospitals. In 1947, persons with mental retardation moved to the Saskatchewan Training School, opened in an abandoned air force base near Saskatchewan Hospital Weyburn. The Training School moved to Moose Jaw in 1955 with 1200 patients. That same year, a group of parents and other interested individuals formed the Saskatchewan Association for Retarded Children, now called the Saskatchewan Association for Community Living (SACL).   This community-based organization became the spokespersons and advocates for children with developmental and intellectual disabilities.   They requested and developed community facilities for education, sheltered workshops and activity centres.  They started group homes and other alternatives to institutionalization.  By 1962, when a second institution opened in Prince Albert, more children were staying at home and in the community.  In 1974, Social Services established the Community Living Services department to coordinate and strengthen health, social services and education for children with Downs Syndrome and other disabilities.[101] As the Saskatchewan Association for Retarded Children developed programs and fundraising, CMHA questioned its role in providing White Cross services to retarded adults.  "If a person has both a developmental and a psychiatric disorder, which should be considered primary?"  Kahan also wondered what "the public reaction would be to CMHA no longer servicing the retarded?"

On another issue, Kahan suggested research into the effectiveness of community treatment.  CMHA Saskatchewan offered grants  for psychiatric research, and Kahan asked for a process for screening grant applicants, particularly in cases where a CMHA board or committee member received funding.  CMHA Saskatchewan needed policy and education statements on suicide prevention, to regulate provision of counseling services generally, and to protest inadequate care in nursing homes and boarding homes.

Kahan pondered the implications of asking government for a monthly stipend for people attending the White Cross Centres.  Would it reduce the appeal to the public if they knew the government was giving substantial funding?  Would it make CMHA less independent and less able "to present submissions which are as forthright and frank if we received government support?"[102]

In June 1968, the CMHA Saskatchewan annual meeting called for planned inspections for the purpose of accreditation of mental hospitals, similar to the accreditation of general hospitals that evaluated the facilities against recognized standards.  Kahan advised Hoffer that the motion to set up a Professional Planning Committee for Hospital Standards specified "that the Committee not include any psychiatrists working in the

Department of Public Health." This excluded several members of the Advisory Scientific Planning Committee. At its July meeting, the Advisory committee responded that "Saskatchewan Division request the provincial government to proceed with the request for a creditation of all psychiatric facilities in Saskatchewan and that the CMHA Saskatchewan Division be informed of the results of these inspections." The conflict of public and professional interests had created a rift.

In the next few months Dr. Frederick J. Gathercole, Director of Education for Saskatoon Public Schools who had agreed to chair the committee, resigned due to work commitments; Dr. Hoffer, psychiatrist and researcher, resigned to devote more time to the Schizophrenia Foundation of Canada;[103] and Dr. A. Stewart, Medical Director at Saskatchewan Hospital Weyburn moved to Victoria. SHW became the Souris Valley Extended Care Hospital. L. A. Morrison was appointed as the new Executive Director for Saskatchewan Division. This shift in the membership and role of the Advisory Scientific Planning Committee marked the end of professional domination in the CMHA. It was two years before the Professional Advisory Committee was revived.

As other areas in Canada and the United States moved toward community care, they recruited the Saskatchewan leaders, usually at a salary that exceeded the PSB rates. With fewer psychiatrists, psychologists and social workers in the province, the burden of mental health care fell on families, on under-trained and under-supervised Approved Home operators, and even on general boarding homes not under the control of the PSB.[104]

The arrest of a former mental hospital patient who murdered nine persons at Shell Lake on August 15, 1967 galvanized public opinion. The PSB appointed Dr. Shervert Frazier to investigate psychiatric services.[105] The Frazier Report in 1968 confirmed that the whole PSB was in the midst of a "personnel crisis"; for example, between January 1 and September 21, 1967 the province lost 13 senior psychiatrists, some junior psychiatrists, and 13 of the 26 staff qualified as Masters of Social Work (MSWs). [106] Frazier supported the Saskatchewan Plan principles but urged slowing down the deinstitutionalization process. Long-term patients leaving the institution required adequate follow-up and resources.[107] Some members of the community were alarmed by the disruptive behaviour of released patients. Although they no longer required acute care, because of their disability or long hospitalization, they lacked social skills or acted in ways that drew unwelcome attention. The public was particularly concerned because people with obvious difficulties were living in the community without any home treatment plans.

> *One brief made the point that early discharge was simply the means to an end, the preservation of the person as a social being; if a patient is discharged to a situation which does not provide for meaningful human contact and social interaction, then one is simply kidding one's self about the merits of early discharge.*[108]

Frazier noted that White Cross Centres were "doing a valiant job, but their resources are often overtaxed." He recommended enriching the social, recreation and therapeutic opportunities in community for "treatment, not just placement."[109]

Frazier's 47 recommendations included an increase in the PSB budget for improved salaries and working conditions for professional staff and an increase in community workers. Patients no longer receiving their residential, occupational and medical services in a hospital required a full range of community services. Approved Home operators requested orientation and training because they were the front line workers with their residents. General practitioners needed more psychiatric consultation and back-up. The move to community care called for more research and training, regular program evaluations and a long-range mental health care plan.[110]

Shortage of personnel, a priority on integrating ex-patients, and a lack of public and CMHA interest in the mental health of children and youth contributed to the inadequacy of services for children.[111]   Frazier said of Children's Programs:

> *There are shortages in virtually every area. The Province has no in-patient facilities for children and completely inadequate clinic facilities. Residential treatment centres are beyond the means of most families, and the procedure under which the Province may pay the cost is generally unacceptable. Counseling and guidance services are inadequate.*[112]

# CHILDREN AND YOUTH MENTAL HEALTH PROGRAM BEGINNINGS

Schools seemed to be the best resource for preventing mental illness and providing normalized support to troubled children and their families. By 1961, the Department of Health employed an educational psychologist in every health region. Beginning in 1947, funding from the Federal Government's Dominion-Provincial Health Grant supported the Educational Psychologist services, at first through the Psychiatric Regions but later through the Public Health Regions. Educational Psychologists and Public Health Nurses worked together to offer mental health services in the natural settings of the school and home.[113] They also worked closely with Speech Therapists and Audiologists.

Educational Psychologists became heavily involved in individual referrals, encouraging families and schools to work together, even modifying school programs to meet individual needs. They also looked at larger issues that affected the well being of students, creating liaisons with other agencies including CMHA and the Canadian Public Health Association. The Saskatchewan Association for the Mentally Retarded and the Council for Exceptional Children programs needed access to psychological services.

In June 1963, the Subcommittee on Services to Emotionally Disturbed Children chaired by Dr. W. G. Bates reviewed provincial services. A brief by Dr. F. A. McKinnon, Director of Guidance and Special Education, Saskatoon Public Schools talked about the importance of early intervention for children with emotional and learning difficulties. McKinnon used an analogy, "while it is necessary to wipe up the mess as well as turn off the tap, more prompt, vigorous and knowledgeable activity at the tap level would mean less mess to clean." McKinnon recommended integrated classrooms with the support needed for students with emotional and learning needs supplied and paid for by public health, education and social welfare departments.[114]

Dr. Alexander Stephen from MacNeill Clinic  enumerated the services for emotionally disturbed children in Saskatchewan.   The MacNeill Clinic, from 1949 to 1968, was the only outpatient mental health service for children and youth  operated by the Psychiatric Services Branch.  It opened in 1949 in a house in Saskatoon under the leadership of Dr. Ray Denson, a child psychiatrist with an interest in learning disabilities.[115]   In 1950, Stephen became the director of the MacNeill Clinic and an outpatient consultant for doctors in Saskatoon and area. He was soon involved in the community, serving as vice-president of the Saskatoon Council of Home and School, lecturing at the University of Saskatchewan on pediatric health and education, and volunteering in other community and professional associations.[116] Doctors Denson and Stephen saw a large number of children because of their interests but they treated adults as well.[117]

Stephen noted that at the end of June 1963 the MacNeill Clinic waiting time was four months or more.  Understaffing and under-funding meant that many children, their families and teachers experienced "minimal service – first aid, after a hurried investigation."  Without suitable support, students repeated grades and experienced undeserved punishment for their learning difficulties.  Stephen asked for more speech therapy, remedial reading, and group therapy. He urged the province to introduce specific teacher training for learning disabilities and emotional disturbances along with in-services for classroom teachers.

Provincial Departments of Corrections and Social Services as well as Health and Education shared responsibilities for mental health care, particularly with juvenile delinquents. Social Services operated the Boys' School in Regina, with 20 beds for delinquent boys under the age of 16 who stayed and went to school for up to a year, but it offered few psychological resources or therapy with these troubled youth.  In the 1960's, the Social Services assumed responsibility for Kilburn Hall in Saskatoon and Dale's House in Regina, both of which had been non-governmental agencies for children who were abandoned, awaiting adoption, or not easily placed into foster homes.[118]

The MacNeill Clinic recommended an additional 15-bed inpatient unit, based on treating 137 children per year for an average stay of six weeks.  If a child really needed hospitalization for psychiatric illness, six beds in the Manitoba Children's Hospital in Winnipeg and up to eight beds in University Hospital, Edmonton were available. In Saskatchewan, 20,000 children needed help, based on an estimate of 10% of the children and youth in the population.[119]

At the same Subcommittee hearing, Dr. Lloyd C. Coates, psychologist with the City of Regina, cited that a study of rural school children around Saskatoon revealed 12% with minor emotional disturbance and 3% with major disabilities. His list of possible service providers to meet those needs included family doctors. Public health nurses already contacted many of these families through prenatal classes, well-baby clinics, parenting classes and immunization programs. Other resources might include social workers with the Department of Social Welfare and private family services. Coates requested more school-based social workers as visiting teachers, plus guidance clinics and mental health auxiliary workers to offer programs for families and schools. He repeated Stephen's argument that children and adolescents who cannot be handled in the home and school required residential treatment.

McKerracher pointed out the severe shortage of child psychiatrists; only 60 of the 800 psychiatrists in Canada spent time in child psychiatry, and of those, only 30 were qualified child psychiatrists. McKerracher noted that there were no guidelines about what constituted adequate services and "no convincing evaluation of child guidance services in Canada, the United States or Great Britain." During the 1950s and 1960s, children and youth were seen as outpatients at the six full-time and fourteen part-time community mental health clinics across Saskatchewan, without specialized staff hired or trained to deliver these services.

Embury House in Regina responded to the need for therapeutic residential care for children and youth with mental illness. It provided 24 beds for children ages 7 to 13 for up to two years' stay. The children were wards of the provincial Minister of Social Welfare, apprehended for "parental neglect", or voluntarily placed by their parents into care for the help they needed. From 1951 to 1955, Dr. Nelson Abraham took on the job of transforming Embury House from a reception depot for children designated as wards of the government into a treatment centre for emotionally disturbed children. He worked with neighbours, service clubs and churches to explain the philosophy of round-the-clock therapy; he emphasized staff training for the house mothers (female) and caretakers (male); he struggled with unions about hours to ensure consistent continuity of the housemothers; and he picked up young theatre goers who broke curfew. To ensure the children got an education, he worked with principals and teachers of four Regina schools. Embury House operated a summer camp at Lebret in the Qu'Appelle Valley offering five or six weeks of ongoing therapy.[120] Embury House closed in 1964 because it served only ten children at a cost of $11,000 per child per year. Eighteen staff transferred to the Department of Social Welfare.[121]

In response to the need for residential services, Dr. Geoff Pawson founded the Ranch Ehrlo Society in 1965. The centre for the treatment, training and education of emotionally disturbed children opened on the Cliff and Julie Ehrle Ranch at Pilot Butte with six male residents.[122] The Ranch Ehrlo philosophy also encouraged community understanding, and research. The workers believed that a child can and wants to do better. Structured living in a residential setting with common sense rules and limits, patience, kindness, honesty and sensitivity helped children be in control. Some children attended schools in Regina for socialization and education. The Ranch also provided half-day schooling with concentration on reading and arithmetic skills.[123]

In 1965, Saskatoon had a school based Child Guidance program, educational psychologists, and a full-time team of two child psychiatrists. Students from Regina were sent to Saskatoon for consultation. MacNeill Clinic found that remedial reading improved emotional health and behaviour. Boys with learning disabilities and emotional problems outnumbered girls by five to one. Effective treatment focused on building skills because research showed childhood pain and failure as a factor in juvenile delinquency. In 1968, the Saskatoon Mental Health Clinic opened with a focus on adult mental health while MacNeill Clinic specialized in the needs of children and adolescents. A summer intern that worked at both the MacNeill Centre and the Saskatoon Mental Health Clinic reflected, "I found that often such facilities do not have a clear idea of the function and responsibilities of the other agencies in the province. ...MacNeill was often regarded as a remedial reading clinic rather than a psychiatric centre."[124]

By the late 1960's, Dr. John Mahon pulled together the Educational Psychology services of the province and cities and helped increase their credibility with school administrators. At the same time, some educational psychologists became teachers when the Saskatchewan Teachers Federation negotiated a better salary schedule than the psychologists.[125]

Until 1970 the educational psychologists trained at the Institute of Child Study at the University of Toronto, which granted a Diploma in Child Study focusing on mental health in education. By 1967, the University of Saskatchewan in Saskatoon developed its own Department of Educational Psychology with an Institute of Child Guidance and Development, and a Department for the Education of Exceptional Children, under the leadership of Dr. John MacLeod. Like Laycock, MacLeod advocated schools, rather than the medical model, for provision of educational psychology, while insisting on the importance of careful diagnosis and medications if necessary. Specialties in Exceptional Children included mental retardation, emotional maladjustment, hearing impairments, language and learning disabilities. The Institute of Child Guidance conducted interdisciplinary research in child development. Also in 1967, the University of Saskatchewan, Regina Campus (which later became the University of Regina) established a Department of Educational Psychology.

In 1968, the Regina Child and Youth Mental Health Services began in the basement of the Regina General Hospital. Dr. Terry Russell,[126] psychologist and the first director, envisioned the service would offer consultation to schools, hospitals, social services and community agencies on behalf of young people and their families in their homes, schools and community. In a proposal to Dr. James Chapman, Regional Director of PSB in 1970, Russell rejected a problem-centred approach in favour of a team approach that would work with other agencies. The team assessed problems, defined treatment plans, and ensured that services were available. He planned a multi-disciplinary clinical approach and a community building 'child guidance' approach, rather than a 'child psychiatry' model. Child guidance focused on supporting children and youth at home, in school, and other programs rather than establishing special residential or school facilities, or psychiatric hospitalization, for children with mental illness.

Regina's Child and Youth clinic specified community consultations and community development in its job descriptions along with more traditional roles of assessment and treatment. The Regina Child and Youth service helped start organizations including The Regina Association for Children with Learning Disabilities, the Family Services Society, and the Rainbow Youth Centre. Staff offered or organized STEP parenting classes. They provided consultation and resources to outreach classrooms and school daycare programs that allowed single mothers to continue high school.[127]   What later became the Autism Society began as a summer family camp when Youth Employment Services (Y.E.S.) students engaged pre-schoolers with socialization and teaching in speech and language.[128]

Over the years, Dr. Russell and his colleagues prepared briefs, reports and recommendations whenever the government announced a new consultation on health and mental health.   They advocated for the whole range of services needed for health, education, and social needs for all children. They called for remedial services for  special needs, including children with mental illness, children in conflict with the law, children with developmental and learning difficulties, and in fact, any handicapped children and youth.   Russell championed comprehensive, multi-disciplinary, regionally based, community-oriented, family-centred Child and Youth programs that enabled early intervention when needed.[129]

By the 1970's, federal cost-sharing supported Saskatchewan Social Services in their child protection mandate with a community program focused on the needs of families and troubled children and youth as well as children with developmental handicaps.  Home support services, foster care and residential treatment were offered through Social Services, the new name for Child Welfare, which had begun in the 1950's.[130]   Ranch Ehrlo received accreditation as a residential community service treating high-risk youth.

A report by The Commission on Emotional and Learning Disorders in Canada (CELDIC, 1970), *One Million Children,* recommended 144 ways to improve the lives of children who needed additional resources. It estimated 12% of children, under the age of 19, experienced mental illness and/or learning difficulties, or were judged to be delinquent or significantly deprived.  CELDIC proposed a comprehensive personal care service to coordinate existing services and to develop new resources in the fields of education, health, welfare and corrections.   Support would be provided for children in their own homes and families where possible, and through group homes as necessary. The school would be involved in the prevention and handling of emotional and learning disorders.  The report called for attitudes of partnership and respect among the various government departments and the front-line helping professions.   It reminded professionals, volunteers and families that they worked together to build on the strengths of the child and remedy the problems. Integrating the services pulled everyone together to treat each child "as a whole person".[131]

In 1971, changes to *The School Act* mandated Special Education classes for handicapped students with funding through the school boards. Funding earmarked for specific children increased the need to test and classify students in order to determine who qualified. A shortage of educational psychologists created a backlog of teachers' referrals. The time spent testing meant less support to teachers, families and children.

Services to children, families and schools in the 1970's were divided between the Education and Health Departments. Ten educational psychologists transferred from the Department of Health to regional offices in the Department of Education to provide assessments on levels of disability. Resources were allocated to school boards on the basis of the number of children with disabilities and the severity of those disabilities. The 'shared services model' allowed smaller school boards to access the pool of professionals employed by the Department of Education. The Department of Health also employed a small number of educational psychologists in a situation that Russell described as

> *four 'early childhood' psychologists for 10 community health regions, no strategy for serving Regina and Saskatoon, no clear program guidelines or direction and no mechanism for integrating these services with other child health services.*[132]

In addition, there were no clear criteria for the designation of emotional and social handicaps. Some educational administrators insisted that only psychiatrists could make that diagnosis. But only three psychiatrists, one in Regina and two in Saskatoon, were identified as child psychiatrists. This shortage limited the number of children identified with mental illness.

In the schools, children with mental illness were grouped with children with behavioural problems. In special education rooms, the resource staff was more attuned to dealing with physical disabilities than emotional issues. Moreover, the legislation on "special classes" did not translate into extra support for students to remain in their home classrooms and schools. Because special classes were only available in the cities, rural parents were asked to agree not only to the remedial class placement but also to a "boarding house" in another community. Not surprisingly, youth who were having problems dropped out of school.[133]

A 1972 re-organization of the PSB saw an overall reduction in personnel and budget. The Community Services Branch of Social Services took on responsibility for the mentally retarded. In 1973, the Training Program for Registered Psychiatric Nurses (RPNs) transferred from the mental hospitals to the Wascana Institute. The re-organization of PSB around various professions increased identification with one's own specialty and reduced inter-professional collaboration. Already over-stretched staff was assigned to particular geographic localities and programs.[134]

At the MacNeill Clinic, referrals came through family doctors. Starting in the 1970's, parents and schools could request services; this change reduced the 'red tape' but increased the wait list for service.

Yorkton Psychiatric Centre ran a busy Child and Youth program. Between June 1973 and August 1974 it reported about twelve new referrals per month and offered in-service sessions and consultation to teachers and schools. On Fridays, the outpatient staff and nurses from the in-patient unit met to assign new referrals to a primary worker who would consult with other professionals. Wednesday meetings dealt with two complete assessments per week, often involving parents and sometimes the child to answer questions and set up programs for treatment. The treatment team included the doctor, psychologists, social worker and community nurses. In a report in *The Saskatchewan Psychologist* (1974), Dr. Don McNeil summed up,

> *Admittedly, members of the Youth Services are not unanimous in what we see as our goal with regard to this service but hopefully we will work out something between the extremes of either withdrawing our services because we are over-extended or on the other side, trying to fulfill the vacancy by the firing of HRPA [the provincial government Human Resource Development Agency] personnel.[135]*

The Alvin Buckwold Centre, a Saskatoon agency for children with disabilities and their families, piloted a demonstration project of home-based interventions with developmentally delayed children and their families from 1974 to 1977. Results of the research on this teaching and support project encouraged the Saskatchewan Association for Community Living (SACL) to expand the Family Support Project to Prince Albert. By 2005, there were 16 Early Childhood Intervention Programs (ECIP) in Saskatchewan. ECIP workers took resources, ideas and teaching methods to the homes of children with disability. They supported families to encourage learning and emotional growth in their children.[136] Later research showed that Early Childhood Intervention, from pre-natal to school age, strengthened social skills, sharpened cognitive function and raised self-esteem.[137]

In 1974, Russell reported that in each of the health regions, children under the age of eighteen who saw a worker from Mental Health Services Branch represented only a small number (from less than 1% to 10%) of the child and youth population of each region.[138] These low numbers suggested that children were not receiving the help they needed in any of the health regions.

Dr. Hugh Lafave, who succeeded Dr. Colin Smith as Director of PSB in 1976, created a committee with representatives from each health region to look at children's services around the province.[139] Looking at the larger picture, Lafave also noted that without adequate community services, re-admission rates for adults with mental illness had exceeded first admissions. The system was not meeting identified needs.

In 1980, the Saskatchewan Prevention Institute (SPI) was founded as a non-profit organization to supplement resources in the government services. SPI set a goal of "healthy children" and a mission "to reduce the occurrence of disabling conditions in children." Their work included research into Early Childhood Mental Health and skill development.[140] SPI sponsored a public-awareness campaign directed toward eliminating alcohol drinking during pregnancy to prevent Fetal Alcohol Spectrum Disorder (FASD).[141] A related organization, the FASD Support Network of Saskatchewan operated a parent-led support group for individuals and families "to recognize themselves as safe, supported, valued and contributing members of the community."[142]

In 1982, the Mental Health Service Branch reorganized around programs: inpatient services, community services and rehabilitation, and children and youth. As provincial Director of Child and Youth Services, Laura Carment began the process of establishing an identifiable Child and Youth Mental Health Service in all regions. She worked to increase coordination among government departments including education, social services and justice and interdisciplinary services within the psychiatric services programs.[143] Eight new staff, half the number requested, increased the capacity of mental health clinics at Swift Current, the Battlefords, Weyburn and Yorkton until each region employed a specialist in child and youth services. The only child psychiatrist worked out of Saskatoon. Neither nursing nor psychiatric nursing training offered specialties in mental health of children and youth, and registered nurses (RNs) and registered psychiatric nurses (RPNs) tended to be under-represented on mental health teams.[144]

Regina Child and Youth Services saw several personnel changes in the 1980s. Dr. David Randall, clinical psychologist, arrived in 1982. In 1986, Dr. Russell moved to British Columbia to become their first provincial director of child and youth mental health services. Dr. James Turanski became the new Director at Regina Child and Youth. Between 1986 and 1987, 12 of 16 clinical positions experienced a change of staff as part of a provincial initiative to reduce the public service. The resulting pressure meant increased waiting lists and restricted services. Laura Carment returned as director of Regina Child and Youth in 1990.

When the federal *Young Offenders Act* (1985) mandated mental health services, two new staff joined Regina Child and Youth Services to provide assessments for court, and to offer consultation and treatment for the Boys' School and Youth Probations. The *Young Offenders Act* challenged Child and Youth clinics in Regina and Saskatoon to complete court-ordered assessments in seven to ten days.

The Regina Child and Youth clinical work emphasized home and community care for children with emotional and psychiatric difficulties. The Regina General emergency and the Munroe Wing in-patient ward were available for consultation, admission as necessary, treatment and discharge planning. Services reached out to support families and allowed children to remain in their homes. When necessary, younger children were placed in foster homes and older youth in approved homes, funded through Social Services. Child and Youth Services offered training and support for the approved home operators. The caseload increased when a number of patients returned to Regina, from Browndale Treatment Centre for disturbed children in Ontario and from Valley View Centre for developmental handicaps in Moose Jaw. Bob Scott, RPN, joined the Child and Youth staff to provide follow-up to this new group of clients.

Department of Education services shared among school districts included social workers, reading specialists and medical specialists. In

1980, the Saskatchewan Community School Program began when a group of Community Education professionals from 16 schools banded together to share information and support and to offer in-service workshops to teachers and school trustees.[145] Community Education encouraged citizens, schools, agencies and institutions to become active partners in addressing education and community concerns by identifying needs and resources to help people raise the quality of life in their communities. In the 1980's, provincial grants to school divisions designated shared services including psychologists and speech therapists.[146]

In 1984, Dr. Tim Greenough, a psychologist, was appointed Director of the MacNeill Clinic.[147] He followed Dr. Colin Lipscombe, a psychiatrist. Greenough changed the emphasis from a medical to a family-centred philosophy, created a multi-disciplinary team, and strengthened partnerships among the mental health services, schools, Social Services and Justice. Saskatoon Child and Youth programs focused on supporting high quality remedial education through support to students, their families and teachers. Staff and programs expanded into the inner city schools. They offered consultation services to day cares. Community development encouraged people with common concerns to support one another and create community solutions.

Dr. Dave Treherne, an educational psychologist employed by Moose Jaw and District Shared Services Organization reviewed the history and current directions of educational psychology in 1984. He called for more early childhood educational programs for children preschool to age seven. He proposed a change from individual funding for students with disabilities to program funding for groups of children. He suggested classes to meet the needs of children who did not function well in the academic setting or who experienced learning disabilities. He supported special education for gifted students. Mental illness required classes for children with emotional and behavioural needs. A reduction in time spent testing individuals would free educational psychologists to establish systematic screening of students. As programs were developed, they needed to be evaluated for their effectiveness in education and support. Treherne foresaw that the computer might mean faster, less time-intensive processing of test results.[148]

The shortage of mental health workers, the needs of children and youth, and the interaction of the health and education departments were among the issues raised in a CMHA Saskatchewan public and professional consultation that resulted in the 1983 report, *The Forgotten Constituents.*

## THE FORGOTTEN CONSTITUENTS

*Dr. Ian McDonald*
*Saskatchewan Archives Board*
*RA-25,035*

In 1983, CMHA Saskatchewan established a Task Force, chaired by Dr. Ian McDonald that examined existing programs and recommended the possible treatment and rehabilitation for people with emotional and psychiatric problems.[149] The final report of the 16-member committee, *The Forgotten Constituents: A Report by the Task Force Committee on the Mental Health Services in Saskatchewan*, covered a full range of community programs. In their consultations, they heard "disappointment, frustration and pessimism" from both users and providers of mental health services. The Saskatchewan Plan had been partially achieved with the two major hospitals phasing out and the regional psychiatric wards established. Few advances had been made since the Frazier Report of 1968. *The Forgotten Constituents* recommended an adequate "supply of community residential settings, vocational rehabilitation and socialization programs to meet varying levels of need".[150]

It flagged a shortage of trained staff for the psychiatric wards, mental health clinics, and community programs. In particular, the Task Force indicated that a shortage of psychiatrists had reached crisis proportions.[151] McDonald warned that as the mental health system broadened its mandate, some professionals preferred to treat "the worried well" rather than chronic "hard-to-manage" patients, "This small group of patients …are shunted from one human service agency to another at great expense in time and energy to families, professionals, the community and indeed to themselves."[152]

Governments across Canada, including Saskatchewan, endorsed "primary prevention" to reduce increasing costs of health care. However, the Task Force did not find evidence of effective practices that reduced the need for active treatment and community services. They also noted a bewildering array of public and private agencies, and asked for directories of mental health services in each region.

Recommendations called for a full range of outpatient and residential mental health treatment programs in each region of the province with specialized services to high-risk groups such as hospitalized children and children of psychiatric patients. Other issues included the age of consent, the need for day cares, adequate funding for foster care, and the rates of teenage pregnancy.

In a 1968 Saskatchewan survey, teachers estimated that 8.4 % of children in elementary schools could be identified as "emotionally disturbed and in need of special programmes." A CELDIC report from 1970 reinforced the teachers' observations:

> *... in any school age population in Canada, the probability is that somewhere between two and three percent of the children are in full-time special educational placements and that teachers, and others, express concern about a further eight to twelve percent of children whose problems in behaviour, self-management or learning are considered to need additional expert help both in and outside of school.*[153]

*The Forgotten Constituents* urged the Department of Education to allocate adequate funding that met the demands for personal counseling for students along with  mental health consultation with teachers and parents.  They advocated adequate funding and resources to assess and meet the needs of children with mental retardation, language disabilities, and social-emotional (behavioural) handicaps.[154]

The Task Force applauded one "bright spot," the government's "commitment and support in the field of research" through the Basic and Applied Studies Units at the PSB. At the same time, it deplored the absence of any public education program that reduced the stigma associated with mental illness.

The Task Force called for greater public awareness and community involvement in mental health planning and delivery. It requested a long-term plan for mental health in Saskatchewan.

The report's *Overview* noted that certain groups, particularly employers, employees, unions and teachers, were under-represented in the voluntary response to their survey. It also expressed disappointment at the small number of consumers and families that responded and called their contributions "invaluable".

*The lack of consumer response represents one of the major obstacles to effecting changes in our service programs. Because of the stigma which still exists in the minds of many about mental illness, patients and relatives are diffident – understandably – about coming forward. Unfortunately, this lack of assertiveness is too often interpreted by the government as meaning satisfaction with, or at least, acceptance of the status quo. In the absence of any information to the contrary, the public may be indifferent or apathetic about those issues affecting hundreds, indeed thousands, of their fellow citizens.*[155]

*The Forgotten Constituents* reported Saskatchewan's call for adequate community programs to "provide needed support for psychiatrically disabled people who are trying to live a more normal life in the community."[156] In the 1980's that group of people began to identify themselves as "consumers of mental health services."

## CONSUMERS AND COALITIONS

The 1980's saw increased consumer empowerment and participation within CMHA. National, division and branch levels called for improvements to the conditions for people with chronic mental illness living in the community. The community mental health literature of the 1980's expanded the scope of support from formal medical treatment to an exploration of social, cultural, and economic factors. It also recognized a need to challenge the feelings of powerlessness in consumers, and often in their caregivers, that resulted from, and contributed to, the impact of mental illness.[157]

In 1982, CMHA National released a book of statistics and recommendations, *Chronic Mental Disorders in Canada* by John Toews and Gordon Barnes. It detailed issues of poverty and income, unemployment and employment among people with mental illness living in the community. It investigated the boarding homes, supportive housing and independent living options in the post-hospital community settings. The role of mutually supportive relationships through families, friends and peer support was a relatively new concept in mental health literature. Although it went beyond the medical model of care, the report also demanded adequate person-centred mental health services.

In 1984, with the Canadian Public Health Association, CMHA compiled an anthology of 36 articles, *Community Mental Health Action: Primary Prevention Programming in Canada.*[158] Among the mental health promotion chapters were essays on starting a self-help group. Instead of being separated from their families, people with mental illness lived at home, coping with everything from childhood to aging. Mental illness often started while young people were still in school and affected the continuity of their education and transition to employment. CMHA National sponsored a series of projects related to wellness in the workplace. And "patient users," who had been hospitalized or treated through a community clinic, told their stories and demanded that the system listen.

The CMHA National Building a Framework project, funded through Health Canada, used those theories and stories to formulate an action plan in consultation with Divisions and branches. *A Framework for Support for People with Severe Mental Disabilities* by John Trainor and Kathryn Church (1984) became a key document for CMHA. It outlined the best ways to approach issues of community mental health care and the empowerment of persons with mental illness.

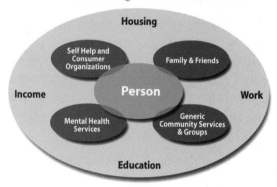

*Community Resource Base  CMHA National*

Central to the Framework was "The Community Resource Base" model which placed the person with mental illness in the centre connected with four main groups: Informal Caring Networks made up of family, friends and neighbours; Self Help and Peer Support; Community Groups and Agencies; and the Formal Mental Health System. This model accepted that individuals with mental health problems could be empowered to control their own lives. It offered choices about the kinds and levels of the supports that met their needs.

The Community Resource Base also clarified the expectation that support could be mobilized in the community beyond the formal mental health institutions, programs and personnel. The Community Reinvestment strategy reminded governments they saved money formerly spent on large mental hospitals. Those savings should be reinvested to ensure people living with mental illness accessed basic necessities for health, security and participation in community. The revised model showed housing, education, income and work as essential elements of a Community Resource Base.[159]

In November 1985, CMHA National *Building a Framework For Support* project organized "Empowerment Through Partnership: A Search Conference on Mental Health Advocacy" at the Government Conference Centre in Ottawa.[160] *From Consumer to Citizen* (1986) documented the three main themes: consumer participation, community reinvestment, and enabling mental health legislation.[161]

At the national level, the Consumer Participation Task Group formed to involve consumers of mental health services in planning and decision-making within and outside CMHA. The National Consumer Advisory Committee (NCAC) established in September 1987 set out to "operationalize the Association's commitment to increased consumer participation at all levels of the Association" and to provide input for consumer nominations to the National board. Their first meeting in 1988 included six consumers representing B.C., Manitoba, Saskatchewan and Quebec and three non-consumer members, two from Ontario and one from Saskatchewan plus a National staff support person.

CMHA National and the NCAC hosted a series of Framework conferences and distributed national policy papers under the direction of Kathryn Church, then Stephen Garnet, and for almost twenty years, Bonnie Pape. The three themes from the 1985 conference were expanded in a series of documents.

*Community Reinvestment: Balancing the Use of Resources to Support People with Mental Disabilities* (1987) dealt with the need to ensure services were available for people living in the community. Saskatchewan had been the first province to empty its hospitals but similar transfers were instigated across the country.

*Consumer Participation: From Concept to Reality* (1988) offered practical strategies to consumers and to CMHA as people who had been recipients of service developed skills and confidence and demanded a place at the board table and as paid employees. For most of its history, the mental health system and CMHA saw people with mental illness as less than capable of managing their own lives, let alone taking leadership and responsibility in the community and CMHA boards.

*Shaping Mental Health Policy: An Action Agenda for Canada* (1988) was aimed at the federal and provincial / territorial governments. Legislation and practice had not changed as consumers in the community demanded choices about access to suitable supports.

In 2004, the Third Edition of *A Framework for Support* integrated previous concepts of community, knowledge, and personal resource bases to support the recovery model. Recovery concepts moved from focusing on problems to recognizing that people with mental illness in the community can live with "success, new challenges met, and a new and enabling understanding."[162]

Although National circulated the research, each Division decided how it would be implemented. A CMHA Saskatchewan board meeting in June 1985 proposed that consumers from self-help groups be invited to serve on the Board or on a liaison committee. The board members wondered whether asking consumers to commit time to the CMHA board would weaken the self-help groups. They debated the problem of "labeling" because "probably a large portion of society ... feels some lingering prejudice." They questioned differences between chronic populations and "members of the labour force that experience a one time mental breakdown ...those who are receiving counseling on a one time basis." They shared concerns that family members declaring their interest might be "an invasion of privacy of the family member who is not involved in the Association." This fear of labeling either families or consumers led to a decision not to designate representation on the board. Rather, the board proposed a plan for cooperation with consumer self-help groups. The discussion paper stated a position that shaped the direction of CMHA in Saskatchewan, and across Canada:

> *No matter what route we adopt, some thought needs to be given to our objectives and mission over the next few years. Self Help groups are coming of age, and a population of consumers is emerging which is not trained in the meek habits of mental patients who have lived in Mental Hospitals all their lives. The changes that such a population is looking for may be as great as the changes resulting from the closing of the mental hospitals.* [163]

CMHA Saskatchewan hosted the 1987 National Conference in Saskatoon, with the theme, "Deinstitutionalization: Empowerment or Abandonment." Five of the 24 speakers were identified in the program as consumers. Eric Braun, founding member and staff of the Crocus Coop self-help in Saskatoon, chaired the first morning. He compared freeing patients from the institutions to the liberation of black slaves, and the consumer movement to the human rights integration movement in the United States. Provincial President Betty Pepper said in her welcoming statement,

> *... the idea grew that by looking at the Saskatchewan Plan we could learn from it and begin to develop a "Canadian Plan" appropriate to the late 1980's. The focus of the Association in the past few years and the participation of more consumers and consumer self-help groups, led us to hope that together in these few days we can develop a vision of a better future.*[164]

Coming out of that conference, CMHA National endorsed consumer empowerment and committed to seeking funds to build consumers' skills and influence in the Association and the community. The Secretary of State of Canada agreed to fund the CMHA National consumer participation strategy. The CMHA *National Framework Project* selected three sites for three year projects beginning in 1987: Etobicoke, Ontario; Moncton, New Brunswick; and Prince Albert, Saskatchewan.

The Prince Albert *Personal Empowerment and Community Capacity* project was based on a joint proposal from Self-Help and Recreation/Education (SHARE), CMHA Prince Albert Branch, Lakeland Council on Social Development, and the Prince Albert Mental Health Centre. These agencies identified the main issues as health, and social and economic support for persons with chronic mental illness. The proposal also called for public policy and a provincial plan to support community mental health.[165] SHARE brought together non-government organizations (NGOs) with interests in mental health, including partners in housing, rehabilitation/recreation and CMHA. About 30 NGOs were invited to an Organizational Mental Health Workshop in Prince Albert in March 1988 "to determine if a Coalition of such a nature is needed to represent the consumer and /or non-government agencies."[166]

A coalition steering committee planned further educational events at regional levels. In January 1988, Arthur Gondziola undertook a four-month contract as coordinator. His first assignment was to increase the representation by family and consumers on the committee from 45% to 51%. He challenged the coalition to strengthen the consumer voice:

> *Members of our Coalition are convinced that if they can strengthen the consumers' voice in articulating their own future*

*Mental Health support needs that they will very directly be strengthening our total health care delivery system. <u>No one can speak as effectively as consumers can on their own behalf.</u> ...*

*Are you up to the challenge of listening to the consumers of the Mental Health service? If you are, you may find that their aspirations, their needs and their dreams are similar to our own ... realistic ... appropriate ... deserving of respect and careful consideration![167]*

By Ourselves drop-in centre in Regina called itself "A Place to Go for Psychiatric Patients" as an alternative, or complement, to CMHA services. Their membership declined the invitation to be part of the Mental Health Steering Committee saying "that we prefer a patient-run council." The letter to the steering committee with the results of the November 1988 meeting added, "Although the membership of By Ourselves certainly want to work in co-operation with other mental health professionals, we feel that control of this committee should rest with the patients who use the services."[168]

In March 1988, CMHA National Framework for Support continued its consumer participation and community reinvestment strategy with a *National Forum on Shaping Mental Health Policy: An Action Agenda.* The Honourable Jake Epp, federal Minister of Health introduced a new blueprint, *Mental Health for Canadians: Striking a Balance.* Strong representation from consumers and families as well as professionals and government officials continued to formulate directions for consumer-centred, community-based services.[169]

At the 1988 CMHA Saskatchewan annual meeting, Division President June Niro promised consumers, "we have not forgotten about you and I will continue to be involved and assist in any way to promote and enhance your participation at all levels of the Association."[170] Saskatoon Branch acted as a catalyst for a family self-help group, The Friends and Relatives of the Mentally Ill (FROMI). In 1988 the personnel and direction of the Professional Advisory Committee (PAC) reorganized with high representation from the University of Saskatchewan and the addition of a family member and writer, Mrs. Byrna Barclay. [171]

Inside the cover:
A Publication of the Mental Health Association in Saskatchewan

*TRANSITION*

Winter 1989

**Special Edition**

A DREAM of Something Better

*1989 Transition Magazine Cover, CMHA
Cover Art by Barry Styre*

Barclay also agreed to edit the *Transition* newsletter and turned it into a magazine featuring writing and art from consumers and family members, branch news and articles by professionals and policy makers.[172] An early edition of the renewed *Transition* featured the CMHA submissions to the Saskatchewan Commission on Directions in Health Care: *The Forgotten Constituents – Revisited* and *A Dream of Something Better – A Proposal for the Planning of a Coordinated and Comprehensive Mental Health System.*[173] Barclay started the provincial Family Advisory Committee (FAC) as a source of information and network of support for families, and to advise the CMHA Saskatchewan board.

In his first Executive Director's Report in 1989, John Hylton highlighted the need for CMHA Saskatchewan to increase funding and membership and affirmed CMHA's commitment to the consumer and self-help movement:

> *The Association has the opportunity to provide a leadership role in contributing to the evolution of the self-help movement. Consumer participation and empowerment must become a reality. Substantial gaps in services in vocational training, employment, housing, advocacy and other areas must be addressed. Prevention programs must continue to be developed and implemented. These are, I believe, the challenges that lie ahead.[174]*

The first report of the Saskatchewan Consumer Advisory Committee (CAC) appeared in the 1990/91 Annual Report, *Building the Dream*. Barbara Evans, the first chairperson wrote:

> *The Consumer Advisory Committee is finally up and running. The committee of Donna Lutcher, Robert Anderson and myself met twice this year and plan to meet again in the near future. ... Arlen Rundvall is organizing the Saskatchewan Consumer Network. We consider this a vital link.[175]*

The Saskatchewan Consumer Network attempted to link existing self-help groups such as Prince Albert SHARE, Saskatoon Crocus Coop and The Regina Club, and also reached out to isolated consumers not connected with self-help groups or CMHA branches.

CAC members indicated a desire to be informed and involved in Division issues including policy, project, education materials and fundraising. The CAC researched income support because pensions for people with disability had the potential to reduce the stigma of welfare. CAC assumed their committee would forge strong links with the Family (FAC) and Professional Advisory Committees (PAC). The FAC identified "professional insensitivity to the plight of families" as a key issue in a list of needs for improved service delivery. The PAC aided negotiations between CMHA and the Mental Health Services Branch; a major issue regarded improving the equality of salaries and benefits between the government and non-government service delivery sectors. They also discussed the need to "improve the interface between the mental health and judicial systems."[176]

Each year the CMHA National Association presented awards that recognized groups and individuals for their contributions to mental health. Saskatchewan placed prominently at the 1990 National Awards Tea. The Prince Albert Nest Drop-In won the Consumer Participation Award; Dr. David Keegan, Chair of the PAC won the Distinguished Service Award; and Dr. David Millar, won the NCAC Consumer Participation Award.[177] Millar, a Regina chiropractor and non-consumer, actively supported consumer involvement at all levels of the Association.

The 1991/92 annual report titled *Stuck on the Edge of Change* launched the Division's new strategic plan and mission statement:

> *The Canadian Mental Health Association in Saskatchewan is a volunteer-based organization which supports and promotes the rights of persons with mental illness to maximize their full potential through education, advocacy, programs, and services.*

CMHA Saskatchewan again called for improved social conditions and a coordinated, comprehensive and community-based range of services " to serve people with mental illness with respect, dignity and quality of life." CMHA committed itself to "ensure consumer and family involvement in Association policies, programs and services."[178]

In 1992, the provincial government announced a new priority for mental health but the increased funding for government services did not reach to increased funding for the non-government agencies. CMHA pointed out that the lack of community services meant hospital admissions remained higher than necessary. It also expressed concern that consumer poverty had "plummeted to tragic depths." The newly created health boards had not asked for CMHA representation. Amidst those setbacks, President Barclay celebrated, "We established a partnership of consumers, families and professionals within the Association that is a first in Canada" at the executive, board and branch levels.

By 1992, branches in the Battlefords, Saskatoon and Yorkton had formed CACs. The Division CAC brought together representatives from the Saskatchewan Consumer Network, the Manic Depression Association as well as CMHA members to discuss health reform, disability pensions, pay equity, and Approved Homes. A highlight of 1991 had been the *Care or Control* conference on "the plight of people with mental illness caught in the justice system." Barbara Evans, Chair of the Division board and Chair of the CAC, challenged the Annual Meeting:

> *I encourage you to continue to make your voices heard, to face the struggles and challenges head on, and most importantly, to rely on one another for support and courage. We have a vision for a co-ordinated, comprehensive system that will deliver health care with compassion and improve the quality of life to those who have experienced mental illness first hand. We must not allow our vision to die. We must continue to work for change because mental illness affects real people.[179]*

The *Making Mental Health Matter* conference in 1994, focused on keeping mental health issues on the agenda during provincial health reform. Staff and volunteers were involved in a provincial government review of the *Mental Health Services Act*. One particular area of interest was the role of Official Representatives, lawyers appointed by the government to help people protect their human rights. Official Representatives assisted people who appealed orders for enforced hospitalization or a Community Treatment Order under *The Mental Health Services Act*. Another initiative in 1993-1994 was a partnership of the SACL and CMHA to address the needs of persons living with both a mental illness and a mental handicap. [180]

After her term as President (1992-1994), Barbara Evans worked for the Division as Director of Branch Development to support the training and planning needs of branches, including strengthening consumer participation. It was a time of change. In 1995, Saskatchewan Health transferred mental health services to District Health Boards so that clinics and programs formerly financed and directed from the provincial Ministry of Health were under newly appointed community boards. Division as a provincial body had related to the Mental Health Services Branch of the Ministry of Health. With transfer to the health boards, mental health policy and programs became less centralized and CMHA branches applied directly to their health regions for program funding. The two largest regions, Saskatoon and Regina-Qu'Appelle, included half of the province's population, provided more than half of the provincial services and were allocated almost 60% of the regional operating costs in the provincial Health budget.[181]   Within CMHA, larger branches including

Saskatoon, Regina and Prince Albert, chose to become more autonomous. Smaller centers, such as Kindersley, Yorkton and Weyburn, retained closer ties with the Division.  In Five Hills Health Region, Mental Health Services assumed operation of the drop-in centre and CMHA Moose Jaw saw an opportunity to undertake new projects.  In the midst of this upheaval, CMHA Saskatchewan moved from shared space with CMHA Regina to a new office.

The Division also started two new programs in 1995. SaskPower provided three-year funding for Friends for Life, "public education and community development to promote mental health and prevent suicidal behaviours."[182]  A new staff member hired for Friends for Life began setting up programs in schools and community groups and building a lending library of resources.

*Friends for Life Logo*

The provincial government contracted CMHA to deliver the Compulsive Gambling Education program.  New CMHA staff based in Regina, Saskatoon and Prince Albert offered presentations and consultation in schools, community organizations, and workplaces. The Compulsive Gambling team celebrated more than 2,000 presentations in its first five years of operations.[183]

In 1995, the CAC negotiated with SGI regarding disability and drivers' licenses; advocated for improvements in Approved Homes; investigated Social Services workers' attitudes toward people with mental illness; and planned advocacy on psychiatric wards.  The CAC took an active role in informing consumers and the public about the Saskatchewan Prescription Drug Plan.

CAC also publicized a strategy, called the Ulysses Plan, that allowed consumers more control over future treatment if their illness became acute and required intervention.  While well enough to make rational decisions, persons with mental illness outlined first and second choices regarding hospitalization, drugs and therapy.  They shared the completed form with people they trusted, their family and mental health team.  The plan specified signs of relapse into acute illness.  If family or friends saw those symptoms, the Ulysses agreement guided their interventions toward the kind of assistance most useful and acceptable to the person with the illness. Similar to living wills, doctors and families made decisions when the consumer was not competent, but they had access to the consumer's preferences.[184]

The CAC's work received recognition when the chair, Donna Gorecki, and another long-time CMHA and Schizophrenia Society volunteer, Doreen Bell, received the 1995 Courage to Reach Beyond award from the Saskatchewan Registered Nurses' Association for "overcoming the obstacles created by their illness to help improve the lives of other consumers."[185]

On a broader scale, a new provincial coalition to foster cooperation among disability organizations started in May 1995 with nine groups including CMHA. At the June meeting, 25 agencies including representatives of the Disabled Person's Reference Group of the Saskatchewan Labour Force Development Board planned how "to bring together individuals and agencies from the disabilities community to discuss issues related to education and employment." A steering committee developed the Provincial Interagency Network on Disabilities (PIND).[186] PIND brought non-government, community-based organizations and labour unions together with provincial and federal departments responsible for training and employment programs with persons with disabilities. PIND consulted with the departments of Post Secondary Education and Social Services because "income security, education, training and employment are inter-related."[187] Two position papers, *Access to Employment Training and Education Funds by Persons with Disabilities - 1995* and *Issues on Vocational Rehabilitation in Saskatchewan – 1996* contributed to redesign of the vocational rehabilitation and the social assistance systems. The network continued to work together to urge implementation and action. PIND succeeded in bringing together a range of agencies to focus on a single area of joint concern.[188]

Ruth Dafoe, one of the first social workers in community mental health, and in retirement an active member of the Schizophrenia Society of Saskatchewan and a member of PIND, was appointed to the Saskatchewan Council on Disability Issues (SCDI) in 1999.[189] The Minister Responsible for Disability Issues appointed individuals with disabilities, parents and services providers. These volunteers conducted 24 community forums in eleven communities around the province to provide advice on issues affecting individuals with disabilities.[190] They presented *The Disability Action Plan* to NDP Premier Lorne Calvert in June 2001. The SCDI visioned "a society that recognizes the needs and aspirations of all citizens, respects the rights of individuals to self-determination, and provides the resources and supports necessary for full citizenship." That concept of full citizenship was affirmed in the Citizenship Statement, "Individuals with disabilities are citizens in the full sense of the term. They have the same rights and responsibilities as other citizens to be included and to participate fully in society."[191]

All sectors of the disability community identified common issues where full participation meant they influenced decisions made for them personally and the policies and systems that affected their lives. People with disabilities wanted access to relevant programs and services with choice and control about how, where, when and by whom those services were delivered. This included opportunities for life-long learning to adapt to changes in the workforce or in their own abilities and interests. People with disabilities wanted smooth transitions from one life stage to another, from children's services to adult programs, and later into senior care. Aboriginal people with disabilities experienced those same issues aggravated by isolation, jurisdiction disputes, attitudes toward disability in their communities, and racism.[192] The *Action Plan* called for awareness and understanding, safety and security, disability supports, health, education, employment, and income support.[193]

The CAC in Saskatchewan suffered setbacks between 1995 and 1997 when consumer leaders needed time to deal with their own mental health issues. However, Eric Braun, a self-identified consumer, was elected President of the Division Board in 1997. The CAC, chaired by Doreen Bell, resumed meetings in 1998 and held four meetings that drew attention to issues including subsidization of medications, the shortage of psychiatrists, the smoking area at the new psychiatric ward in Regina, Community Treatment Orders, and investigation and advocacy with specific individuals. The next year the Committee looked at policies in Approved Homes, especially the integration of their clients into community programs.

In 2001, the CAC had become inactive. A new CMHA Saskatchewan Advocacy Committee mandated "to support and advise Division on advocacy issues brought forward by individuals, families and branches ... [to] promote standards and services to meet the needs of the individuals and families who experience mental illness" included consumers. They took leadership on the Advocacy Committee and with the Mental Health Coalition in consultations and presentations related to the provincial Fyke Commission on Medicare, and the national Romanow Commission on the Future of Health Care in Canada. Consumer participation was being built into the fuller mandate of CMHA Saskatchewan.

A provincial *Commission on Medicare* headed by Kenneth J. Fyke (2001) was appointed by Saskatchewan Premier Roy Romanow. When Romanow left provincial politics, he headed the national *Commission on the Future of Health Care in Canada* (2002). Both Commissions warned about the fragility of Medicare and called on health providers, governments, and the public to focus on their obligations to create a sustainable system.[194] Both paid scant attention to the human, social and medical costs of mental illness.

Fyke recommended an integrated model for the delivery of primary health services with, for example, a province-wide telephone health line. He noted that mental illness disables about 12% of the population and quoted A. Pirisi who wrote in *The Lancet* medical journal:

> *While first-world nations have been tackling diseases such as cancer and heart disease, and less developed nations have been waging a battle against malnutrition and AIDS, mental illness has sat on the backburner around the globe in terms of medical and public health attention and resources.*[195]

Fyke proposed "a province-wide plan for the location and delivery of specialized services based on standards established by a Quality Council." He included psychiatry as one of the specialist sectors offering education, consultation/supervision, with research and evaluation.[196] He concluded that education and research were essential to the process of change in the health system.[197]

*The Commission on the Future of Health Care in Canada Report* (2002)[198] also focused on the sustainability of health services, going beyond doctors and hospitals to include home care and a national drug strategy.[199] Romanow described mental health as the "orphan child" of health care and made one recommendation related to mental health home care: "Improve the quality of care and support available to people with mental illnesses by including home mental health case management and intervention services as part of the *Canada Health Act.*[200] To meet the goal of lowering medical costs, home care case management and co-ordination of services for persons with chronic illness, and home intervention in acute episodes reduced the need for hospitalizations. These services would have also reduced the burden on families dealing with mental illness, Alzheimer's disease and dementia.

Romanow stated, "mental health care remains one of the least integrated aspects of health care." He said that deinstitutionalization too often meant that a person was abandoned or returned to a family who had to provide care with very little support. Years of isolation in institutions affected not only the patients but also raised the fears and prejudices of the public. He observed that fifty years after patients moved out of the mental hospitals, lack of support for individuals and their families, stigma and discrimination still remained. For people with severe and chronic disability, this undeserved sense of shame was increased by attitudes against people who needed income assistance.[201]

Income support and individualized funding for people with disabilities were on the table at the April 2006 *Putting People First Forum* hosted by SACL. The "Coalition of Disability Advocates working to improve the income support system in Saskatchewan" shortened its name to DISC (Disability Income Support Coalition). CMHA asked DISC to address the episodic nature of some disabilities. For example, people with mental illness or multiple sclerosis have times when their condition is very limiting and other times when they have more energy.

Email technology supplemented meetings to share ideas, vent frustrations and develop consensus on common language among agencies and the essential issues to take to government. The emails showed significant input from individuals living with disabilities as well as community organizations.[202] DISC presented a united appeal to the Ministry of Social Services for recognition that people with disabilities have ongoing needs and requested a disability income plan. The program administered through Social Services, but separated from the short-term income support program, offered more dignity and benefits to people with disabilities. The Saskatchewan Assured Income for Disability (SAID) enrolled their first group of eligible persons (persons already living in residential care) in December 2009. The PIND/DISC partnerships continued to work for increased exemptions on earned income and inheritance, and incremental increases in benefits. When Social Services opened the program to people with disabilities living in the community, PIND held open houses to provide information and assistance with the application process. Volunteers assisted individuals to complete the paperwork that Social Services required to move their files from Income Assistance to SAID.

CMHA Saskatchewan in its 2010-11 annual report declared that community collaboration with significant consumer input continued to "encourage the Government to ensure that there is an adequate level of support to make a meaningful difference in the lives of those needing this support" [203] for empowerment, choice, and access to adequate resources.

Some people need the support and services of a secure facility for longer-term treatment, for assessment and rehabilitation. Saskatchewan Hospital North Battleford is the only provincial mental hospital. Construction began in 1911 and the first patients arrived in February 1914. In 1955, the population reached 2,043. The 2011 census included a few long-term patients, a forensic ward and a youth rehabilitation ward, totaling 156 patients. In 1994, the Forensic Unit was set up for people with mental illness in long-term detention, and for persons accused of a crime who must be assessed before proceeding to trial or sentencing. Over the years, the Mental Health Coalition, the RPNAS, and various professional and community groups have called for the replacement of the obsolete and decaying institution. In August 2011, Saskatchewan Party Premier Brad Wall announced a modern hospital with 188 beds to be built on the same grounds. The bathrooms would no longer be down the hall and shared by a dozen patients. Single rooms would allow more privacy and living space.[204]   In August 2012, the construction had not yet started. SHNB treated young adults, dealing with mental health and addictions issues, who needed longer-term rehabilitation unavailable in outpatient or regional psychiatric facilities.

## MORE PLANS FOR CHILD AND YOUTH SERVICES

To meet the mental health needs of children and youth involved services that spanned the education, justice, social services, and health ministries. Addressing needs such as parenting, poverty and child care were part of the process. Building safe and supportive communities where people felt a sense of belonging reduced high-risk behaviours. Early intervention in episodes of mental illness increased the potential for recovery as the person received adequate and effective treatment. A brush with the justice system indicated an opportunity for mental health intervention. This chapter looks at some of these factors.

The Saskatchewan Department of Education *Action Plan for Children* introduced in 1993 addressed the cycle of poverty, prevention of Fetal Alcohol Syndrome, and best ways to support early developmental needs of all children. *KidsFirst,* a voluntary program assisted parents of preschool children through home visits and community services to build on strengths for parenting and healthy child development.[205] With federal funding, *KidsFirst* began operation in eight selected communities in southern Saskatchewan and in all the northern communities.[206]

In 1994, health administration transferred from the province to health regions. In the process, Child and Youth Mental Health Services, formerly MacNeill Clinic, became a department of the Saskatoon Health Region and the Regina Child and Youth became a department of the Regina-Qu'Appelle Health Region [RQHR]. In other regions, child and youth mental health services received more or less attention depending on the leadership and staffing.

The National Crime Prevention Strategy, initiated in 1994, did not directly link with mental health issues. Rather, it addressed risk factors in high-risk populations and communities through social development.

Families and schools provided youth with opportunities for involvement that fostered competency and participation skills. Improved functioning in school and work lowered rates of criminal behaviour, and reduced symptoms of anxiety and suicidal thoughts.[207]

In 1995, Ranch Ehrlo Community Services expanded beyond the residential care for high-risk youth to the provision of accommodation for low-income families, support for single mothers, sports programs, career development, and outpatient counseling services. They aimed "to provide quality programs to vulnerable youth in Saskatchewan and beyond, through social treatment and advocacy, of benefit to the individual, family and community." [208]

Jo Anne Phillips, director of Regina Child and Youth Clinic reported about 2,000 cases each year in their outpatient service. Her 1999 newsletter article added that this "is just a fraction of the number of children in RQHR that could benefit from specialist mental health services." Children with mood and anxiety disorders, and disruptive behaviour including attention deficit hyperactivity disorders (ADHD), and eating disorders accessed the services. Children as young as two years old were diagnosed with severe, moderate or mild mental illness. In Canada, suicide was the second leading cause of death among young people aged 15-24 (second to accidental injuries) and suicide was the third leading cause of death among 10-14 year old children (after accidental injury and cancer). Phillips emphasized that mental illness must not be blamed on parents but the whole family must be involved in the treatment plan for children and youth.[209]

In 1999, The Saskatchewan Mental Health Services Branch introduced Early Psychosis Intervention (EPI) in Saskatoon for the northern half of the province. Psychosis is a symptom of schizophrenia, bi-polar disorder or other mental illnesses. The patient appears out of touch with reality, sometimes experiencing delusions and hallucinations (ideas, visions, voices or sensations), and may have difficulty thinking and speaking coherently.[210] Persons, ages 15 to 30 years, experiencing a first episode were referred by a family doctor or psychiatrist. The program attempted to reach the person within 72 hours for rapid evaluation. Treatment and rehabilitation for the first two years such as assertive case management maintained contact to ensure that the patient used medication as prescribed. Parents, teachers and the patient received education about the disorder and coping techniques. The program's psychiatrists and community mental health nurses offered individual and group sessions.[211]  In 2006, EPI  expanded to Regina for the southern part of the province.  The traditional dividing line was at Davidson.

In February 2001, a report to the Minister of Education of Saskatchewan by Michael Tymchak, the Chair of the Task Force and Public Dialogue on the Role of the School, introduced *SchoolPLUS – A Vision for Children and Youth, Towards a New School, Community and Human Service Partnership in Saskatchewan.*  The Task Force recommended that all schools adopt the Community School philosophy.[212] A Community School incorporated four components: the Learning Program; Family and Community Partnerships; Integrated Services, and Community Development.  Together these elements addressed complex social, emotional, health and developmental issues with links to community resources available within and beyond the school.

In 2002, Saskatchewan Learning offered the *Children's Services Policy Framework* to meet the diverse needs of children in family, school and community.[213] It assisted school divisions to develop policies, programs and services to support all students.   Health-related services included "therapeutic, consultative and counseling services provided by mental health workers, physical and occupational therapists and support personnel" collaborating with schools and families.  In 2004, 98 schools with approximately 36,000 students and their families, half of whom were Aboriginal, used Saskatchewan's Community Schools Program.[214]

In the early 2000's, Saskatchewan Health expanded existing services in various health regions and agencies. More personnel were hired in Child and Youth Mental Health Services.  The Randall Kinship Centre, Regina, opened in April 2002 to provide treatment and support to families when a child had disruptive behaviour problems. In 2004, a new psychiatric wing at the General Hospital in Regina added an inpatient unit for adolescents.  Professionals and

*Face in a Building, Nyla Raney*

para-professionals in children's mental health received additional training in evidence-based practices, autism intervention, and research methods to measure mental health outcomes.

Youth from birth to nineteen years made up more than 25% of Saskatchewan population in 2005. In that same year, this age group used about 11% of total mental health services. This disproportion raised the question whether children and youth underutilized or lacked access to mental health services.[215]

Social Services operated residential resources for youth-in-care including Dale's House in Regina, Red Willow Centre in Saskatoon, and the Prince Albert Grand Council Education Centre in Prince Albert. Therapeutic or treatment foster homes helped "young persons living there to deal with some of their fears, issues and behaviours that are causing them problems."[216] The Calder Centre Youth Program in Saskatoon, a 12-bed residential unit provided services for adolescents and families dealing with substance use and abuse.[217]

The Saskatchewan Children's Advocate Office (CAO) report in 2004 specifically addressed mental health issues. *It's Time for a Plan for Children's Mental Health* reiterated the CAO 1996 and 2001 concerns about child and youth access to mental health services.[218] It looked back at *The Forgotten Constituents* (1983) and said, "The recommendations made by the McDonald Task Force are still relevant today." [219] The CAO offered a working definition of mental health:

> *the capacity of a child or adolescent to meet culturally normative developmental milestones by engaging in activities of normal development, fulfilling relationships with other people, and the ability to adapt to change and to cope with adversity; from early childhood until late life, mental health is the springboard of thinking and communication skills, learning, emotional growth, resilience, and self-esteem.[220]*

*It's Time for a Plan* also summarized the mandate of Child and Youth Mental Health Services:

> *The purpose of child and youth mental health services delivered through health regions in Saskatchewan is to promote, preserve and restore the mental health of children and youth directly through the provision of care and services, and indirectly through the support to other service sectors involved with*

*children and youth.[221]*

CAO recommended the development of a plan with multiple strategies to serve the diverse needs of children, adolescents and families. CAO also called for a research plan for collection, analysis and evaluation of statistics on the needs of children and youth and the services that best meet those needs. Both the provincial Department of Health and the Regional Health Authorities would have a part in the collection and evaluation of data.

As a result, Saskatchewan Health conducted consultations with a range of stakeholders:

> *Learning, Corrections and Public Safety, Mental Health Services, child psychiatrists, parents of children and youth with mental disorders, Alcohol and Drug Services, primary health care physicians, family physicians, nurse practitioners, public health nurses, Community Resources and Employment, Ranch Ehrlo Society (community-based organization), Aboriginal services, youth (Aboriginal and non-Aboriginal), adults of an Aboriginal community, Justice, Youth Court judges, and Early Childhood services.[222]*

The results, *A Better Future for Youth:  Saskatchewan's Plan for Child and Youth Mental Health Service* (2006) recognized that 15% of children and youth lived with functional impairment in daily living because of mental illness while another 15% of children and youth were vulnerable to mental health problems. There were not enough mental health professionals to meet these needs. *A Better Future for Youth* advised a "multiplier model" so that some treatment was provided directly, but the professionals also supported parents and school services to build on the clinical interventions. To alleviate the pressure on families, *A Better Future* recommended children's mental health respite services. The multiplier model depended on building partnerships with other sectors and organizations providing services and supports to children, youth and families. The Saskatchewan Mental Health Services plan did not call for systematic research to evaluate whether the multiplier model met the needs of children and youth and their teachers, parents and caregivers. [223]

The Canadian Institute for Health Information (CIHI) published *Improving the Health of Canadians 2008: Mental Health, Delinquency and Criminal Activity.* It emphasized "that while most people with mental illness do not commit crimes, youth and adults with diagnosed mental illnesses are over-represented in Canada's correctional facilities."[224] Anxiety and aggression affected about 10% of the Canadian youth surveyed in 2004-2005. Half the youth aged 12 to 15 reported fighting, attacking and threatening people, bullying or property destruction. Males were more likely than females to engage in aggressive and destructive behaviours.[225]

The same factors that promoted good mental health also reduced delinquency and risk of violence. CIHI used an American study to illustrate that healthy and supportive environments improved the safety and health of children. Children and youth who felt loved, wanted and trusted by their parents, accepted and connected at school, secure and valued in the community and who enjoyed optimism about their future were less likely to be aggressive or engage in risky behaviours.[226] The report drew attention to the links between mental health factors and delinquency but added "few policies and strategies, particularly those for which evaluations have been conducted, address factors specific to mental health and crime prevention simultaneously."[227]

Rates of depression, anxiety disorders, attention-deficit hyperactivity disorder (ADHD) and substance abuse disorders were higher among youth in custody than among young adults in the general population. Youth in custody were also diagnosed with conduct disorder, post-traumatic stress disorder (PTSD), and schizophrenia. Almost all inmates could have benefited from help with substance abuse and emotional issues. While about 4% of the Canadian population was Aboriginal in 2002, the Canadian prison census reported that 17% of men and 26% of women in correctional facilities were Aboriginal. Aboriginal inmates tended to have lower rates of completed education, lower employment histories, higher rates of unstable housing, higher rates of repeat offences and higher rates of violent offences.[228] Aboriginal mental health concerns required action with cultural sensitivity.

Child and Youth Services in health regions stretched to meet mental health needs. Community mental health workers in the clinics around the province were available for consultation and support. Psychiatrists and other professionals at Child and Youth Services in Saskatoon and

Regina specialized in child and adolescent psychiatry and worked with family physicians, schools and other community agencies. Where possible, parents and guardians were included in the treatment team and parent education was a part of the care plan. Treatment options included behaviour therapy and addictions counseling. Child and Youth offered crisis intervention. Adolescent inpatient units, at the Regina General Hospital, and in the Dubé Mental Health Centre opened in Saskatoon in 2010, offered hospitalization to stabilize acute psychosis by starting medication and other therapies. Community development, including sensitivity to First Nation and Metis culture, values and beliefs, created alternatives to meet specific needs.

A *Maclean's* Special Report in March 2011 commended Saskatchewan for its delivery of services to children and youth, and reflected initiatives outlined in the 2006 plan:

> *It includes parent mentoring and "preventive intervention programs" at 16 sites across the province for vulnerable children under five years old, and outreach programs in Aboriginal communities. In Saskatoon, psychologists and counsellors work from inner-city schools. Mental health is part of a larger "school wellness initiative" where speech pathologists, occupational therapists, nurses and counselors work together. In addition, addiction workers operate in the inner city, says Rob Strom, coordinator for community and youth addiction teams in Saskatoon. "Our workers are helping our clients get to appointments, get hooked up to the right services, taking them out for lunch or coffee, building relationships."[229]*

Finding and accessing the right services for yourself or a loved one often entailed a time-consuming and frustrating search. *The Incredible Parent Directory 2009/2010*, a resource booklet for parents and professionals within the City of Saskatoon included an index of approximately 325 resources. The agencies, government services, and websites were sorted into sections such as addictions, bereavement, crime and justice, education, housing, parenting, special needs, separation and divorce. Such a long list emphasized the fragmentation of the "system" and the need for a wholistic strategy for mental health. The guide, published on the Saskatoon Health Region website, was compiled by several agencies. Service providers submitted their descriptions; listings did not imply screening or endorsement of any programs.[230]    That directory, and sources in other communities or websites, channeled some users into an appropriate referral or service.  Otherwise, after countless phone calls, families contacted CMHA because they could not find the help they needed.  CMHA shared their frustration and advocated for services that fit the client individually and on a systemic basis.

Many people of all ages who needed mental health support did not receive appropriate care.  Steve Lurie, executive director of CMHA Ontario, was quoted in the *Maclean's* magazine: "In Ontario, basically one in three adults get access.  If you are a child, it's one in six."

## ISSUES FOR AN AGING POPULATION

Since the 1960's, people living with chronic or episodic mental illness usually accessed treatment through community care.  By 2012, there were few survivors of institutionalization in large hospitals.  People with mental illness, hospitalized for safety and stabilization during a crisis, returned to their homes, jobs and community.  When a person presented a danger to self or other, or was likely to deteriorate if not hospitalized, they could be admitted to a psychiatric ward.  If necessary, a Community Treatment Order enforced regular medication, usually through a needle, and regular contact with a mental health worker.  Some people fell between the gaps in the system with their mental illness disguised as people who were in prison or homeless or afraid to leave their apartments.  For most citizens with long-term mental illness, health was maintained through medication, therapy, lifestyle decisions and a range of family, friend and mental health support.

This group of persons with a life-long experience of community mental health had aged in the community.  Depression in seniors needed to be recognized and treated as an illness, not written off as a sign of aging.  Dementia presented both physical and emotional challenges for the person, and the caregivers.   The "baby boomers," born 1945 to 1965, have had a demographic impact at every stage of their life journey.  Aging citizens expected a continuum of quality and appropriate physical and mental health care services.  A CMHA Saskatchewan project, *Iceberg on the Horizon: Mental Health Among Older Adults: Social, Intellectual, Spiritual (MH-OASIS )* sounded an alert that the baby boomers were approaching seniors status.  This 2003-2006 project advised health care and community resources to prepare for the changing needs of older adults with mental illness.  Physical disabilities and health concerns also affected people with mental health problems.[231]  Older adults  presented a complex range of needs to be coordinated through physical, psychiatric and geriatric care. Primary care was usually delivered by general practitioners and home care workers, some of whom still believed depression was normal in the elderly population. Workers more concerned with the physical aspects of care could be inexperienced when dealing with mental illnesses. A nursing supervisor in one senior care home admitted, "I'm more comfortable with bed pans than panic attacks." Community mental health services seldom followed individuals into geriatric care in public or private nursing homes.

Fifty years of community mental health in Saskatchewan had not erased misunderstanding and stigma surrounding mental illness and persons who experience mental illness. Aging carried its own stereotypes and devaluation of personhood. Older adults with a chronic mental disorder often faced poverty issues. They coped with the usual age-related losses in vision, hearing, mobility and physical health on top of the challenges of living with a mental illness. Grief and isolation impacted all seniors with the possibility for depression, especially among people who have a history of mental illness. On the other hand, a sense of being needed and belonging in family and community improved quality of life. Seniors still needed the basics of income, housing, good nutrition and transportation.

Consumers, family members, volunteers, and professionals who participated in the CMHA survey expressed an interest in programs and services to meet the diverse needs and interests of older adults with mental health challenges. Mental health advocates had not been particularly aware of seniors' issues. Leaders in some seniors' organizations expressed surprise that mental health is an issue for older adults. Seniors' recreation and mental health social recreation programs were encouraged to find ways to work together. Leaders in mental health and in seniors' issues shared similar hopes for respect, wellness, and appropriate resources to meet the health and social needs of the aging population.[232]

A follow-up report by CMHA in 2010, *Beyond Barriers – to Participation: Recreation for Older Adults with Mental Illness*[233] encouraged access to recreation that enhanced physical, social, spiritual and emotional health. Participation benefited society as well as the individual. The 'healthy aging approach' valued and supported the contributions of older people and celebrated diversity. Age-friendly environments for older Canadians enabled healthier choices to enhance their independence and quality of life.[234]

Persons most affected by aging and/or mental illness wanted to be involved in the planning, implementation, and evaluation of any program. Other people, agencies, and government were urged to support and encourage participation in cooperation with (not for) older adults with mental health difficulties. Older adults wanted to be recognized for their wisdom, life experience and common sense. Seniors who participated in this CMHA Saskatchewan *Beyond Barriers* research specified that older adults are "not problems, but problem solvers."

"A reason to get up in the morning" was a common concern expressed by people who experienced depression and loneliness. On the other hand, more than one senior spoke about needing an appointment book to record the variety of social, recreational and volunteer activities of each week. One 80-something woman summarized her busy calendar, "I used to go to work and come home, but now I have something different to do every day." Participation in a whole range of activities that enhanced physical, emotional, spiritual and social wellbeing were essential to health at any age.

*Mental Health in Long-Term Care  CMHA, Debb Black*

# SOCIAL RECREATION PROGRAMS IN SASKATCHEWAN
## 2011

CMHA Branches placed a high priority on their social recreation programs since the early days of the White Cross Centres.  Around 1971, the White Cross Centre name was dropped and the programs were identified by community names: CMHA Weyburn, CMHA Regina, and so on.  Drop-ins that had been named by members didn't change: The Regina Club and the Prince Albert Nest.  As consumers developed skills and autonomy, they took more control of their programs and services. Crocus Coop in Saskatoon, a long-term self-help project, provided drop-in, a lunch program and programming run with and for people who experience mental illness.  SHARE (Self-Help And Recreation Education) in Prince Albert formed its own Board and programs, although many people participate in both SHARE and the CMHA Nest.[235]

CMHA Kindersley retained its centre of attention on public education, advocating for mental health services and working with other agencies from the 1970's when they pressed for a local mental health clinic and the 1980's when they supported community development of West Central Crisis Centre.  Kindersley did not take on direct service projects.

Every branch worked at education and advocacy on behalf of individuals, improved services for people with mental illness, and healthier living conditions for all citizens.  Most branches focused on pre-vocational and social recreation programs funded through the health regions.

Starting in 2005, health regions promoted the "recovery" model as a further step in helping people with mental illness to gain more autonomy and independence. Recovery-oriented planning responded to the goals and intentions of the consumer instead of slotting clients into existing programs. Changing the philosophy and format offered possibility for transformation for individual consumers, and also for the program staff and the programs. Recovery literature recognized that people want to live full and meaningful lives. Service providers were empowered to help people with mental illness to set goals and work toward them.

> *Recovery refers to the ways in which a person with a mental illness and/or addiction experiences and manages his or her disorder in the process of reclaiming his or her life in the community.*

> *Recovery-oriented care is what psychiatric and addiction treatment and rehabilitation practitioners offer in support of the person's recovery.*[236]

If a consumer wanted to participate in a marathon, write a book or get a job, the recovery-oriented worker helped the person break the task into manageable objectives, suggested ways to get started and offered ongoing encouragement to continue. Depending on the current level of fitness, a member joined a walking group as a starting point for a marathon. Participation in a writers' group built skills and a community of support for the book project. The vocational programs at most CMHA branches prepared clients for paid employment. Larry Davidson, a leader in schizophrenia recovery research, emphasized, "Many people think having a job is a lot of stress. Not having a job and not having enough income is even more stressful."[237]

Davidson, director of the Program for Recovery and Community Health at Yale University, spoke at a 2008 conference in Regina. He described transformation of the whole service provider and consumer perspective because "recovery cannot be simply the latest thing we <u>do to</u> people with mental illness."

> *Recovery <u>from</u> refers to eradicating the symptoms and ameliorating the deficits caused by serious mental illness, while being <u>in</u> recovery refers to learning how to live a safe, dignified, full and self-determined life in the face of the enduring disability which may, at times, be associated with serious mental illnesses.*[238]

Building resilience, recovery and community implied availability of a continuum of options for treatment and everyday life. To ensure the person had a meaningful choice, the community and the mental health system needed to prepare to respond to the decisions and desires of the consumers. Davidson asked service providers to examine their motives as well as their actions in working with people with mental illness. He proposed this question, "Does this person gain power, purpose (valued roles), competence (skills), and /or connections (to others) as a result of this interaction?" He pointed out that recovery-based programming does "more of what works" to build upon the skills, resiliency, confidence and competence of members so that every activity enhances recovery.[239]

The Recovery Model, like the CMHA consumer empowerment and consumer participation *Framework for Support*, assumed that people with a disability had the strengths, wisdom and desire to improve their situation even when they needed support and assistance "to live a full and meaningful life." Program directors and facilitators, who started with an attitude that everyone had the human right to hope, healing, empowerment and inclusion, created what recovery literature called a "positive culture of healing." A pre-vocational program prepared people for the vocational program and/or encouraged people to balance work and leisure time.

The Regina Branch reported the goals and achievements of their 2009 recovery-oriented pre-vocational program:

*The Pre-vocational Program strives to provide a welcoming, engaging and accepting environment where people coping with long-term mental health concerns can develop a social support system, and focus on ways to stay well. The Program's philosophy is to create and provide opportunities for meaningful involvement, and non-structured activities (i.e. recreational outings and a variety of fitness activities, crafts, baking, music groups, local entertainment tickets, one to one support and small groups, education, advocacy, crisis intervention, etc.). Our activities change from month to month as they reflect and address client needs. Often, these activities aim to expand people's connections in the community. The drop-in centre, or THE CLUB, was open daily (except Stat holidays) and very well utilized. Our goal is to empower individuals to be resilient, to focus on their strengths, to develop good coping strategies, and to work towards self-determination.* [240]

Each month, branches with social and vocational programming planned a calendar of activities including seasonal and birthday parties. Physical exercises were scheduled regularly, a wide variety of activities from yoga and stretching at the Centre to swimming and bowling in community facilities. Activities to build skills for daily living included hands-on cooking, sewing, computer use and education sessions on healthy living. Groups on relationships, anger management and assertiveness training added communication tools. In Regina, that was called the TALK Group (To be Assertive but Listen to be Kind). Leisure activities included card playing, movie afternoons and gardening. Forty to fifty members attended the monthly dances in the Battlefords; popular demand had returned dances to the monthly schedule. For all CMHA programs, choice was named as a value. No one was forced to participate. A person chose whether or not to take part in any of the scheduled or spontaneous activities.

A social recreation and pre-vocational program based on a recovery model went beyond setting up a calendar and letting people decide whether or not to attend. A recovery-based program asked what individuals wanted and explored the strengths, abilities and aspirations of each person. Action plans were client-centred and built on personal interests and goals. A recovery-based system transformed as it worked with people as individuals and/or as groups with shared goals towards the attainment of each person's aims. This involved collaboration with community and mental health agencies.

The level of involvement by the formal mental health system varied from branch to branch. Mental health workers, usually psychiatric nurses or social workers, referred their clients to the CMHA community-based recreation and vocational programs. Many branches allowed people to come without a referral. In some branches, the community mental health nurses visited clients at the centre on a regular or drop-in basis. In other cases, branch staff met with mental health workers to share concerns and care plans. In most branches, consumers supplied the name of a relative, friend, or worker who could be contacted if staff were concerned about them.

Most people with mental illness lived in their own homes or apartments, alone or with family, while a few lived in supported housing or group homes. In the Battlefords, where many of the older members lived in Approved Homes, CMHA and the home operators needed to maintain good communication and coordination regarding mutual expectations on issues such as programming and transportation. Branches sometimes helped people find and keep adequate housing. In some cases, that meant organizing work crews to deal with cleaning and clutter that threatened to overwhelm the person, or the landlord. Some, though not enough, supportive housing programs for people with mental illness operated in Regina and Saskatoon.

The number of branch program participants who were employed seemed to depend on the availability of employment in the community, the ages and the severity of disability of the members. Many of the members in Swift Current and Moose Jaw centres were employed at least part time in the community. In other communities, such as Weyburn and the Battlefords, the members were unemployed, but the Branch pre-vocational program contracted odd jobs like snow clearing or lawn mowing. When Weyburn members felt ready to seek employment, they were referred to Weyburn and South East Services (WASES), a community employment service that helped with vocational preparation such as résumé preparation, job search and interview skills. Prince Albert ran several projects that employed members, explained in more detail later. Regina and Saskatoon offered a formal vocational preparation program with life skills and employment coaches who ran courses, arranged field trips to potential employers, and offered support as people entered the workforce after a long-term disability or an episode of illness. Regina members earned work experience in the kitchen and canteen, and the Branch opened a Laundromat in cooperation with a mental health housing project.

Most branches charged the annual $2 fee for CMHA Saskatchewan consumer membership that granted voting privileges in the Branch and Division annual meetings and a subscription to *Transition* magazine. The $10 per member per month in Swift Current covered the breakfast and lunch programs, drop in, and other costs of bowling, pool hall, swimming, and events tickets. Most branches used grants and fundraising to pay for activities and events. Because poverty was an issue for many of the consumers who used their services, branches often subsidized the costs of programs and community participation. Sports clubs and cultural events provided tickets to be distributed to consumers. Approaching potential donors, writing grant applications, and organizing fundraising events were essential skills for CMHA staff and boards.

Meal programs were important. Swift Current served breakfast for five to ten people and lunch for about 25 people five days a week. The breakfasts started at the request of psychiatrists who advised food with morning medications. Weyburn staff and kitchen crew worked together on topics like meal planning and budgeting and "meals from scratch" to reduce the use of processed and prepared foods. In Swift Current, the Battlefords and Regina, meal programs added benefits of improving nutrition and encouraging participation among the members. Often the skill-building of a job in the kitchen to prepare and serve food was a step in vocational preparation for the workers.

The CMHA Prince Albert service contract with the regional health authority supported drop-in, vocational, and support services. The Nest drop-in, open Monday to Friday, attracted 60 or 70 people each day, some for most of the day and some just for a short visit. Some of the 150 members of the drop-in came every day and some came occasionally. The Nest ran a vocational program with 35 people on the payroll for one to thirty hours per week. The Good as New store sold used clothing. The Homestead Quilting workers designed and constructed recycled fabric into quilts sold across Canada. People who worked in these projects received a small honorarium, because earnings beyond $125 per month were clawed back by Social Services. When people were ready to leave a family home or group home to live on their own, they accessed the independent living program that prepared and supported persons of any age, with education for the decisions, tasks and responsibility of renting an apartment, buying groceries, paying bills, and enjoying leisure constructively.

Many of the activities planned by branches added interest and enjoyment to members' lives. Local musicians and groups were invited to provide entertainment. Swift Current members expressed interest in opportunities to explore different kinds of music from country to jazz through listening and if possible, with special guests. CMHA Regina attracted musicians who practiced and performed with The Free Spirit Band and entertained at several nursing homes as well as at The Club. The "Just Having Fun" Harmony Group learned the art of barbershop singing and performed for special events at The Club. The Regina Reel Anti-Suppressants theatre group developed skits and performed for various locales (schools, conferences, and community events) to educate and entertain around issues that affect people with mental illness.

A CMHA Saskatchewan project, *Healing through Humour* ran a series of sessions preparing consumers to develop and perform sketch and stand-up comedy. Each series ended with a public performance. It was not intended as therapy but Ian Morrison said of himself, "even the guy who runs the program has an illness." Course members were encouraged to take care of themselves and if they missed a week, they were welcomed back. The objective was not to cause anxiety but to ease anxiety. People brought different skills and learning styles; they learned together how to create and present their talents as performers and members of a community. Morrison pointed out that people could be both highly functional and severely ill; finding the right job on a workable schedule allowed them to maximize their potential. Morrison reassured participants that just getting on stage is something most "normal" people do not dare to attempt. And since people needed to laugh, he reminded the comedians that they played an important role in society.

The Saskatoon Branch offered a writing program beginning in the mid 1990s. In 2009, Ted Dyck, Saskatchewan author, editor and educator obtained funding through a Saskatchewan Arts Board Exploration Grant and developed a pilot project on therapeutic writing groups. He also edited the CMHA Saskatchewan publication, *Transition*. This little magazine had a history of publishing articles, stories and poetry by consumers. Dyck contacted CMHA branches in Swift Current, Moose Jaw and Weyburn to set up or expand their writing programs. A volunteer in Prince Albert also developed a writers' group. Writings from these groups appeared in the Spring 2010 and Spring 2012 issues of *Transition*. Dyck concluded,

> *Anecdotal evidence that writing for therapy contributes effectively to the recovery-oriented, community based delivery of mental health services is accumulating. ... writing helps to develop, empower and articulate a Self that has too long been stigmatized both for itself and as an unfortunate burden on society. But the Self with direct experience of mental illness that emerges from the writing in these groups is, in my view, a very special representative of the human condition that measures all of us.[241]*

Art programs with classes in drawing, painting and other mediums, along with opportunities for personal creations, were popular in the Swift Current, Weyburn, Saskatoon, Battlefords and Regina branches. For several years the CMHA Saskatchewan prepared a fundraising cal-endar featuring artwork submitted by consumers around the province. Members received payment for their art-work. CMHA also paid a commission for the sale and delivery of the calen-dars in the cities and rural areas.

*2013 Fundraising Calendar,*
*CMHA Saskatchewan*

Summer programming offered the pleasures of a day trip or short holiday to consumers who might miss out on that experience. "We live on the edge of lake country," said Doug Kinar, CMHA Prince Albert, "but some of our clients from the city have never been to the lake, never been fishing." A day at the lake, a barbecue and time with friends in the great outdoors created treasured memories and anticipation for next time. Most branches organized special activities, day trips, even five-day tours or camping experiences and assisted their members to attend community festivals and participate in seasonal fun. Some-times volunteers from Katimavik or other cultural exchange programs added flavour from another area of Canada or the world.

CMHA Saskatoon made extensive use of volunteers. Recreation Coordinator Sandy Stotz held membership in the Administrators of Vo-lunteer Resources (AVR-SK), a provincial volunteer management group. All the recreation programs were organized and conducted by volun-teers. CMHA benefited from its membership in Volunteer Saskatoon, a service that posted volunteer opportunities. New volunteers were con-stantly being recruited to provide new programs and to allow flexibility for activities and the volunteer leadership. Stotz was responsible for the job descriptions and recruitment. People who indicated an interest were interviewed, reference-checked, and trained in preparation for running their programs. She also kept statistics on programs and participation.

Stotz said that client intake interviews for the social recreation pro-gram were quite informal although the conversation could take up to an hour. Entry into the vocational program was by referral by a mental health worker, but people self-referred into the recreation program. The interview focused not on the person's illness, but on the person's interests. The interviewer asked, "What do you like to do? What do you want to do? When and where?" The client intake interview served as an ongoing source of information for planning programs. Sometimes the programs were offered by CMHA but as often as possible, the clients were encouraged to enroll in a community program that suited their needs. CMHA Saskatoon preferred to run programs in normal community settings. Members played basketball and volleyball at the YWCA from October to the end of May, and enjoyed swimming during the summer at one of the outdoor pools.

The recovery-based programs emphasized the desires and interests of the clients. They developed activities for constructive use of leisure time for people who had employment as well as for people who used more of their time and energy to cope with the illness. Programs ran in the evening or on weekends to involve people who had jobs or took part in the vocational preparation sessions. After two months of participation in one or more of the CMHA activities, members were interviewed about their experience. Then they received a courtesy card to participate in all activities at CMHA. A newsletter and calendar were distributed every month or two on paper and through the CMHA Saskatoon website.

Every three or six months, the volunteers evaluated their programs. They asked participants what worked (or not), talked about what could be improved or tried, and again, gathered ideas for other programming. These findings were reported to the volunteer coordinator who used this opportunity to encourage and support the volunteers.

Some schools allowed credit for volunteer service, usually five hours in a term. The Volunteer Saskatoon website advertised opportunities for high school students to get experience in the CMHA social recreation program. Students were recruited as participants, not leaders. They engaged socially with the clients by taking part in one or more of the regular groups. At the end of their experience, Stotz met the students and asked them to reflect on what they had experienced. She inquired what they thought before they started and how their perception of people with mental illness had changed after time with them. High school students, or their friends, can be at risk for depression, anxiety, eating disorders or the onset of schizophrenia. Stotz asked, "After your experience here, is there anything different that you would do now to help yourself or someone you know who may be experiencing mental health issues?" Students' answers indicated that volunteering helped them understand more about mental illness and reduced fear and stigma.

Many programs took a break in July and August while a summer student developed the branch summer program. This gave the regular volunteers a holiday. Some eager volunteers, retired people or students who were not working, continued through the summer months. One of the consumer members of the writers' group took on the responsibility of opening and locking up the building, making the coffee and ensuring the space was open and welcoming for the group.

Every couple of years, Stotz planned a consumer consultation to talk about all the programs at CMHA, inquiring about leisure and recreation interests. Participants evaluated the activities, and brainstormed potential programs. Volunteers facilitated breakout sessions at the consultation to ensure that all the ideas were heard. If there weren't enough registrants for a consultation, consumers filled out a survey or were interviewed to give feedback on past and future programming. Not every idea was possible, but all ideas were considered, and sometimes a volunteer came along just at the right time.

When CMHA Saskatoon received a donation of fabric, Stotz asked

*The Recovery Quilt for the Dubé Centre, CMHA Saskatoon (2011)*

the CMHA branch at Prince Albert about their quilting group. Saskatoon quilters volunteered to help piece a large Recovery Quilt to hang in the Les and Irene Dubé Psychiatric Inpatient Centre at Royal University Hospital. Participants from the McKerracher Centre, the Crocus Coop, Saskatoon Housing and CMHA worked together. Some of them told their stories of hope and recovery during the presentation of the quilt to the Dubé Centre. Stotz recalled that public storytelling as "a good moment for social recreation in Saskatoon."

CMHA purchased supplies for quilting and other projects such as scrapbooking. Volunteers brought new ideas and good energy to their groups. Quilting and conversations go together naturally, or as one member said, "Quilting means community." Quilters met one week and scrapbookers the next week. Thus, volunteers were scheduled every second week. Some members attended both activities.

Another faithful volunteer came every Thursday to make popcorn for games or a movie, and when the weather was nice, encouraged a group walk. Volunteers at CMHA Saskatoon modeled the pleasure and satisfaction of watching people have fun, gain confidence, and grow in their ability to enjoy their lives.

Consumers who did not want to take full responsibility for running a program assisted the volunteers. Sometimes success in a leadership role developed the kind of confidence that led to more volunteer opportunities in the centre and the community, or to the vocational program and employment. CMHA Saskatoon offered pre-vocational and vocational programming, with two vocational counselors, a job developer, and a life skills coach, and shared the volunteer coordinator with the recreation program. The Branch recovery employment programs did not focus on the psychiatric diagnosis but concentrated on what people wanted to do, where they wanted to work, and what support they needed to be successful. Funding for the program staff and activities came from the Saskatoon Health Region, United Way, grants from the Saskatchewan Parks and Recreation Association and fundraising.

Stotz said that rules were kept simple and discussed as necessary. For example, one rule specified zero tolerance for alcohol or drugs; that had not been a problem. The emphasis was on absolute respect in language and actions of members, staff and volunteers.

Respect was expected in drop-in and organized programs at all branches. The recovery model emphasized mutual respect, listening, empathy, compassion, safety, trust, diversity and cultural awareness. A recovery-based program did not over-protect consumers by trying to eliminate all stressors but provided opportunities for safely testing abilities, learning new skills, developing resiliency, and enjoying the satisfaction of accomplishment. Respect meant trusting, encouraging, and expecting that people lived up to their best hopes, dreams and goals.

Full citizenship included the right to self-determination in everyday life as well as in the treatment and rehabilitation of illness. Full citizenship meant social inclusion regardless of resources and despite symp-

toms and functional impairments. The recovery movement sought transformed communities where individuals were assisted to live full and
meaningful lives through connections with the social, recreational, educational and vocational activities of his or her own choice. Suitable and
timely supports were available as long as needed but no longer than
needed.

CMHA Moose Jaw experimented with a different model after their
health region grant no longer funded the branch drop-in and social programs.  Starting in 2002, the Branch concentrated on educational and
community programs from their office in a community school.  Donna
Bowyer, the executive director helped form a group for families living
with Asberger Syndrome, a form of autism.  The experiential learning
program offered family support and assisted young persons to acquire
practical skills such as cooking, budgeting and social interaction in community settings.  Another project in cooperation with the Multicultural
Council, the schools and other community agencies helped multi-cul-
tural youth starting high school to avoid drugs, addictions and gangs.
Youth and their families explored their aspirations for education and employment.  Family activities assisted integration into the community.

Donna Bowyer defined her job as involvement in the community to
maintain public awareness of mental health.  At the provincial Partners
Against Violence conference calls and in-person meetings, she spoke
about bullying as a mental health issue.  In all her interactions, she emphasized the importance of trust and safety and the values of respect and
resilience. CMHA Moose Jaw approached City Council to draw attention to local suicide rates and the need for police education to deal with
people with mental illness.

The Come Together consumers operated as a peer-support group
funded by the health region through CMHA Moose Jaw.  Darrell Downton acted as co-chair of the self-help group.  The co-chairs and members
established  and enforced the rules, planned the activities, and set a positive tone for their monthly meetings.  They usually met at a restaurant
where they checked in about what is happening in their lives and families.  The Come Together members volunteered for CMHA fundraising at
the community bingo hall.  Over the years, participants learned the skills
and gained the confidence necessary to assume full responsibility for ensuring enough workers to cover the shifts.  Come Together members no-
ticed that people who took on responsibility had fewer hospitalizations.

Some members progressed to competitive employment as they learned to deal with the stress of working. When there were problems, the team called a lunch to resolve the difficulties. If invited, Bowyer acted as support and resource person. Downton encouraged other health regions and CMHA branches to consider supporting consumer-run groups and projects to develop leadership skills for fuller consumer participation. After several years in branch activities, Downton was elected in 2009 as President of the Division Board, chaired the provincial Mental Health Coalition and served on the Mental Health Commission of Canada (MHCC) Peer Support committee.

Donna Bowyer spoke of her satisfaction when people who felt they couldn't do anything took on more responsibility, or found a regular job. She noted that people with mental illness are everywhere and there's no need for stigma.

> *Twenty years ago, people with mental illness were wrapped in bubble wrap and protected from the community and even from each other. Now they are recognized as people who happen to have an illness. With education, see how they have blossomed.*

Bowyer also forecast that the role of community mental health programs continued to change as many people with mental illness used electronic social networking skills to build their community of friends around their hobbies and passions.

The majority of people with mental illness who required medical treatment never participated in programs run by CMHA or other agencies specifically dealing with mental health issues. Most people with mental illness were busy with jobs, families and hobbies. They made friends through church, service clubs, and community activities, sports, theatre, gym, quilting, wood carving - the many activities that are available in towns, cities and rural areas. In other words, citizens with mental illness benefited from, and contributed to, the many social and recreational avenues of our society.

Bowyer worked part-time in the Saskatchewan Division *Friends for Life* program. Workshops for *Friends for Life* and *Mental Health First Aid* helped people identify potential problems and set up protocols and policies for offering help. Usually Bowyer invited a consumer to accompany her for presentations at schools and community groups to illustrate that people in recovery were capable contributors to society.

The programs of CMHA Saskatchewan should be re-evaluated against the framework principles of recovery, choice, community and integration proposed by the MHCC. The *Patient First* philosophy, proposed by Saskatchewan Health, promoted creative, client-centred programming. Broad national, provincial and local strategies created potential pivot points for CMHA and other mental health service agencies. These ideas will be explored in the next chapter.

# CHANGING TRENDS AND STRATEGIC DIRECTIONS

At its 2002 annual meeting, CMHA Saskatchewan reviewed its history and re-imagined its future.[242] Members compared the budget to the stated aims of the Association. The budget allocated more than three-quarters of staff time and money to direct service provision through the vocational, social and recreational activities of the branches. Public awareness and education, a stated priority, received a fraction of total resources. CMHA no longer funded research into the causes of illness or best practices for rehabilitation. Advocacy, the original reason for CMHA, held the smallest piece of the pie. Families and consumers came to the Division and Branches for advice and assistance when the system did not meet their needs.[243]

Executive Director Dave Nelson drew attention to three stated outcome measures for CMHA Saskatchewan. CMHA's success would be measured by the quality of life for people living with mental illness. It promoted good mental health and prevention of mental illness through its own programs and through other agencies and government services. CMHA supported human rights for everyone including people with lived experience of mental illness. The Division re-affirmed a commitment to looking at the whole mental health system and continuing to work toward a comprehensive, coordinated strategy for promoting mental health and serving the needs of consumers and families.

*The Conway Report* of 2003 studied the mental health workforce in Saskatchewan, not specifically the community-based voluntary sector.[244] It compiled comprehensive profiles of various professions which provided mental health services.[245] It also reviewed "issues, needs and gaps in mental health services" and recommended ways that workers could better meet client needs.[246] The report noted a shortage of evidence-based treatment programs for mental health in Saskatchewan in many areas, both by specialty and by geography, along with the need for more public education and mental health promotion.

Consumers told John Conway clearly that family and friends were essential to their recovery and coping. Families and consumers recommended community development work "to initiate and sustain voluntary and informal support networks."[247] Conway called the voluntary sector "bridge builders," advocates for change to improve the lives of people with lived experience of mental illness. But the lack of funding and a focus on rehabilitation services reduced CMHA resources available for public education and advocacy.[248]

In August 2007, CMHA partnered with Saskatchewan Health and Saskatchewan Advanced Education and Employment to look at the role of community-based organizations (CBOs) in mental health. In the *Mental Health Sector Study,* CBOs evaluated the process of seeking and maintaining health region contracts for specific direct service programs. It reduced their ability to push the Regional Health Authorities and governments for policy change. On the other hand, the grants were essential for CBO operations to provide needed programs for people with mental illness.[249] The narrow definition of direct service in the funding agreements left out many of the other aspects of their response to the complex needs of individuals living with long-term mental illness. A number of CBOs, including CMHA, were funded for social interaction and support programs, pre-employment and employment preparation. Housing projects offered another specific service. Some agencies also offered counseling and support services through individual and group sessions. Another direct service involved assessments and referrals to other agencies.

Through the *Mental Health Sector Study,* fifty-six CBOs identified major gaps in the mental health delivery system. Service providers, directors of Mental Health Services, and post-secondary educators echoed the survey findings. Almost all expressed concern about staffing in their organizations. Community, voluntary, non-profit sector employees received a much lower wage than government employees doing similar work. Lower pay and benefits increased the difficulty in hiring and keeping qualified mental health workers in non-government services. Meanwhile, funders expected more service without increasing grants. CBOs felt caught in a moral dilemma because if they did not offer the services, people living with mental illness suffered. Succession planning in organizations often fell to the bottom of the priority list until a key employee was no longer available.

Most agencies identified a need for public education about available resources and first points of contact. For example, mobile crisis services operated in Regina and Saskatoon and the Saskatchewan HealthLine had mental health workers on call but people in crisis might not know where to start. CBOs suggested education about specific illnesses, depression, schizophrenia and bi-polar disorders, in the school system and for the public. They noted the lack of Regional Health Authority directives for education programs to address mental health issues. A visit to a doctor, psychiatrist, mental health worker or a community agency did not necessarily link the person or family with other services. There were no clear paths for referrals and access to resources. Adequate, affordable and effective supports were scarce and overburdened. Needs were unmet; suffering and suicides resulted. Moreover, an unknown number of people who could have benefited from services and support never requested help because they did not know it was available, or because they feared the stigma of mental illness. Other factors, such as personal and geographic isolation or the shortage of trained service providers, also presented barriers.

Several agencies requested a new diploma level program to prepare people for work in a variety of positions in the mental health field. Front line workers in the formal system and community-based organizations repeated the call for a long-term mental health strategy to link the government and non-government agencies in a comprehensive support system for people with mental illness and their families.[250] CBO staff and funding often stretched for general overhead, community participation, and responses to other unmet needs. Without an adequate base funding the advocacy mandates of prevention, health promotion, public education and coalition building were left without specific resources and personnel. Cooperation and collaboration suffered when short-term contracts ended and staff changed.

A provincial strategy for mental health was needed to address concerns in health regions, community agencies, professional and para-professional education. In particular, the CBOs called for a collaborative and comprehensive system for people who need and use the mental health services and support.[251]

Across Canada, *Out of the Shadows at Last: Transforming Mental Health, Mental Illness and Addiction Services in Canada* (2006)[252] by Senators Michael J. L. Kirby and Wilbert J. Keon raised the profile of mental health issues. Subsequently, the federal government appointed the Mental Health Commission of Canada (MHCC) with a ten-year mandate (2007-2017) to provide direction for mental health policy through provincial / territorial and federal governments as well as individual and community action.

Mental Health Commission de
Commission la santé mentale
of Canada du Canada

*MHCC Logo*

*Out of the Shadows* built on the experience of people with lived experience of mental illness. The first two chapters reflected what the Committee heard as they traveled across Canada. "Voices of People Living with Mental Illness" quoted stories about the impact of symptoms, social conditions and stigma. "Voices of Family Caregivers" raised the key role of family members in providing care while feeling excluded and ignored by the formal services. "Persons with direct experience of mental illness" were upheld as key informants. *Out of the Shadows* focused on the concept of "recovery." The person, not the system, determined which services and activities were most appropriate at any point in time. The person, not the system, set the direction for mental health policy and service delivery.[253]

Originally, "living in the community" meant the opposite of living in an institution. The Saskatchewan Plan in the 1950s and the CMHA *Framework for Support* of the 1980s expected that services would be available close to people's homes. Quality of life required adequate housing, income, work, social connections and mental health services and supports (both formal and informal). Integration set the goal of a variety and a continuum of activities and services for people at different stages of their illness, different ages of their lives, and when possible, as part of the same services and supports available to all citizens.

The MHCC set as its objective "to keep mental health issues in the mainstream of public policy debates" across federal, provincial, territorial, municipal governments, and among the various ministries within each government as well as in public services, workplaces and community settings. [254] Through nation-wide consultations with stakeholders, the MHCC developed a mental health strategy published in 2009, *To-*

*ward Recovery and Wellbeing: A Framework* for government use in developing their own policy and programs for mental health.   The MHCC
had no authority to make policy.   Provincial governments with their departments of health and social policy remained responsible for planning,
implementing and evaluating the directions and infrastructure for service
delivery and community support.   However, MHCC developed a series
of projects and initiatives to illustrate and inform change.

The MHCC described itself as "a catalyst for transformative
change" influencing the attitude of Canadians "to help people who live
with mental health problems lead meaningful and productive lives."   The
*Changing Minds* media and anti-stigma campaigns researched the best
ways to change attitudes.   They arranged opportunities when persons
who lived with mental illness were in direct contact with specific groups
and the general public through face-to-face and media encounters.
Sports figures, entertainment stars, and other community leaders seen as
successful and high functioning spoke about their struggles with mental
illness.   Stories of everyday ordinary people showed that recovery was
possible.

Before the MHCC mandate expired, *Partners for Mental Health*
launched an ongoing initiative as a non-profit organization. Starting in
April 2012, *Partners* began publicity and fundraising to develop a social
movement toward mental wellness in Canada.   They focused on success
stories. Another campaign identified that everyone has some bad days,
but some people have them every day.   Normalizing "bad days" was intended to encourage people to seek help for recovery and coping with
mental illness.

The mental health system was not  the usual first point of contact for
children, youth, adults and seniors with mental health problems. Before
they approached their family doctor or emergency room, they usually
talked to friends and family, teachers in schools, leaders in their faith or
contacts in social networks.  MHCC introduced *Mental Health First Aid*
training for frontline workers in community agencies and schools as well
as mental health providers.   *First Aid* taught skills to help people respond to someone with a mental health problem or crisis.  Like first aid
in a physical crisis, the mental health first aid addressed immediate dis-
tress and danger of suicide, and assisted the person to get appropriate
help.

Homelessness remained a mental health issue. The *At Home/Chez*

*Nous* pilot research project in five cities offered housing and services to 1,325 persons. Living in an affordable, supportive environment created an atmosphere of safety to free the person's energy for other issues -- from addictions and therapy to education, work and community involvement. Interested groups and individuals accessed web-seminars to follow this housing experiment.

Across the country and internationally, there were examples of creative, successful ways of solving problems and improving the lives of people with lived experience of mental illness. The whole health system pushed the concept of "best practices" tested and shown to be effective and practical. The MHCC *Knowledge Exchange Centre* was designed as a central source of information about mental health and best practices for the various stakeholders and issues in this complex field.

Eight MHCC advisory committees conducted research and pilot projects. Some committees were based on the life cycle:   Child and Youth; Seniors; and Family Caregivers. The First Nation, Inuit and Métis advisory group investigated this often overlooked population with attention to historic and current conditions and the complex issues of jurisdiction, governance and cultural sensitivity in the delivery of services. Mental Health and the Law recognized that a multifaceted justice system constantly connected with persons with mental illness -- police called to homes for domestic violence or threats of suicide, juvenile delinquency, and inmates in prison because suitable supports were lacking.   Prisons offered the equivalent of the former mental asylums - custodial care without treatment.

The Science Advisory Committee reinforced research and evaluation in developing practices for effective and efficient mental health delivery. The Science committee committed to engaging a network of consumers in investigating and analyzing the complexities of mental illness and mental health. The Science Committee also ensured that research reflected the multicultural aspects of mental health service delivery.

The Service Systems Advisory Committee acknowledged that the supports and services for people with lived experience can be delivered by people with a wide range of skills and experience.  Peer-support and consumer-directed services as best practices deserved a place in comprehensive mental health care.  The Workforce Advisory Committee was concerned about the working conditions of all citizens because employment, unemployment and working conditions exerted a significant impact on mental health. It also focused on the best kinds of support for people with mental illness in the workforce, and with the mental health needs of service providers in the mental health system.

Each advisory committee, with teams of researchers and policy advisors, examined current conditions and innovative responses. The MHCC Child and Youth Advisory Committee estimated that 70% of adults who live with mental illness reported that their symptoms began in childhood or early adolescence.[255] The MHCC released *Evergreen: A Child and Youth Mental Health Framework for Canada* in July 2010 after consultation with young people as well as families and workers in the field. The Child and Youth strategic direction addressed four categories: promotion of mental health, prevention of mental illness, suitable and adequate intervention and care, and ongoing research and evaluation.[256] The recommendations were intended to assist governments and agencies in developing child and youth mental health policies and practices.[257] Other MHCC advisory groups recommended policy changes in their areas of expertise, with reports published online as they were released.

Saskatchewan Health formulated the concept of *Patient First* in October 2009. *Patient First* insisted, "it is time to realign the values of Saskatchewan's health system so that the patient is again made the center of attention." [258] This contrasted with a system based on the convenience of people who provide the services. The Commissioner, Tony Dagnone, reviewed the health system and recommended *Patient First* embedded as a core value in a well-integrated system. Front-line providers were empowered to deliver patient- and family-centred care.[259] These goals meshed with the client-centred, consumer-directed objectives of the recovery model for mental health.

*Patient First* promoted collaboration among the government, non-government and community agencies and activities that offered support. In Saskatchewan, the Ministry of Health plus thirteen health regions plus various health care organizations and independent practitioners offered distinct or overlapping services. Lack of a coordinated approach created difficulties for persons trying to get help. Dagnone said, "This quasi-network of somewhat independent agencies and professionals must begin to think and act as one system for the benefit of the patients."[260] The report concluded, "For the sake of patients, [Patient First] must become a movement that is embraced by all who have a stake in creating healthier communities." [261]

In Regina and area, a Steering Committee from education, municipal governments, police, community agencies and Regina Qu'Appelle Health Region conducted a multi-year interaction with stakeholders around a strategic approach to mental health needs. After two years, an independent consultant's report, *A Call to Action – A Mental Wellbeing Strategy for Regina and Area* (2012) highlighted that 20% of adults and 15% of children and youth experienced mental illness each year.[262] People with chronic illness absorbed most of the system's available time and resources. The service providers also reported insufficient resources, lack of coordination among providers and agencies, and a shortage of health promotion and illness prevention education. The draft strategy proposed "making the most of what we have" to allocate resources strategically. It also directed "increasing quantity of services through increased resources," in other words, increasing the budget for service delivery. Service providers were encouraged to "maintain high standards of service that are responsive to client need." The recommendation to "better serve the needs of First Nations, Metis and Inuit people" acknowledged the wholistic philosophies and teachings of the Aboriginal peoples.[263] To achieve those key directions, *A Call to Action* asked for the voluntary commitment of all who contribute to the system.

The Saskatchewan Mental Health Coalition meeting in November 2011 reviewed *A Call to Action* and urged moving toward a comprehensive mental health strategy for the whole province. At Coalition meetings, organizations and individuals shared their current concerns. With resources from CMHA and the Schizophrenia Society of Saskatchewan, the Coalition expanded its membership of agencies involved with helping people with lived experience of mental illness. The SACL and CMHA partnered to gather and share information with families whose children have complex physical and intellectual disabilities as well as mental health issues. Anecdotal accounts warned that children with emotional problems had not received services because their needs were not severe enough, despite obvious difficulties for the children, their families and teachers; the full weight of care overburdened family members. As a child moved from the youth services to adult services, the *Privacy Act* prevented professionals from giving (and in some cases receiving) information from parents and caregivers who were still expected to monitor and support their family members. Thus, one meeting illustrated several recurring issues in the fragmented history of mental health in Saskatchewan.

CMHA has persisted as one of a number of organizations promoting education, self-help, advocacy and service for mental health. Many other organizations arose to fill needs around specific diagnoses (Schizophrenia, Anxiety Disorders, Autism and many others) or specific services (housing, drop-in, employment and so on.) The MHCC, various provincial initiatives, the Mental Health Coalition and a whole series of reports urged a coordinated, comprehensive strategy for mental health.[264] CMHA has enjoyed a history of forming partnerships and coalitions, leading the way in advocating comprehensive and visionary strategies for change, and involving families and consumers along with professionals and government leaders in shaping policies and programs.

CMHA at all levels again reviewed its mission and structure in the changing environment. "Strengthening Our Collective Impact: A Strategic Plan for CMHA" was the theme for the Na-

Canadian Mental Health Association National Conference
October 18 & 19, 2012     Delta Regina Hotel, Regina, Saskatchewan

tional annual conference in Regina in October 2012. The Strategic Plan, approved by the National Board in February, had three goals: "strengthening the CMHA voice, ensuring quality services, and enhancing the organizational structure governance model."[265] CMHA as a voice with and for people with lived experience of mental illness along with mental health service providers offered a resource and balance with the policy makers and system managers. It maintained a focus on recovery and person-centred care that valued choice, community and integration. CMHA continued to advocate, activate and evaluate services to meet the needs of people with mental illness and those who cared about them. As a national Association, working in provincial and territorial Division structures, and through branches in local communities, CMHA's collective voice made a difference in the lives of people with lived experience of mental illness. This is the history and future of the Canadian Mental Health Association.

# APPENDIX A
# CMHA SASKATCHEWAN PRESIDENTS 1950 – 2012

| PRESIDENT | TERM |
|---|---|
| Dr. Samuel R. Laycock | 1950-1953 |
| Mrs. A. Davidson | 1953-1956 |
| Mrs. N. P. Toombs | 1956-1959 |
| The Ven. F. E. R. Badham | 1959-1962 |
| Mr. T. H. Cowburn | 1962-1966 |
| Mr. A. R. Riddell | 1966-1968 |
| Mrs. A. M. Derby | 1968-1969 |
| Rev. James A. Beairsto | 1969-1971 |
| Rev. R. M. Thompson | 1971-1973 |
| Mr. A. Gonziola | 1976-1978 |
| Mrs. T. Busse | 1978-1980 |
| Mr. M. (Mel) McCorriston | 1980-1983 |
| Mr. Dave Millar | 1983-1985 |
| Mrs. Betty Pepper | 1985-1986 |
| Mrs. June Niro | 1986-1988 |
| Mr. Robert (Bob) Burrage | 1988-1990 |
| Ms. Byrna Barclay | 1990-1992 |
| Ms. Barbara Evans | 1992-1993 |
| Mr. Len Broten | 1993-1994 |
| Ms. Rose Morris | 1994-1997 |
| Mr. Erskine Sandiford | 1997-2000 |
| Mr. Eric Braun | 2000-2002 |
| Mr. Jim Beach | 2002-2003 |
| Ms. Sharon Lyons | 2003-2006 |
| Ms. Susan Grohn | 2006-2009 |
| Mr. Darrell Downton | 2009-2012 |
| Mr. Grant Rathwell | 2012-2014 |
| Ms. Sharon Lyons | 2014-2016 |
| Mr. Chet Hembroff | 2016- |

# INDEX

A Better Future for Youth..................**107**
A Call to Action.................................**136**
A Strategic Plan for CMHA...............**137**
Abbott, Anne.......................................**23**
Abraham, Nelson................................**73**
Action Plan for Children....................**103**
Advisory Committee on Medical Care **57**
Agnew, Neil.........................................**28**
Alvin Buckwold Centre.......................**78**
Anderson, Robert.................................94
Anthony, William A.............................**62**
Approved Homes. **49, 55, 64, 97, 99, 119**
At Home/Chez Nous..........................**133**
Autism.........................................**76, 137**
AVR-SK (Administrators of Volunteer
    Resources)....................................**122**
Barclay, Byrna.............................**93, 95**
Barnes, Gordon...................................**87**
Bates, W. G.........................................**71**
Battlefords (see also North Battleford)
    .........................**11, 80, 95, 118pp., 122**
Beers, Clifford....................................**23**
Bell, Doreen.....................................**98p.**
Beyond Barriers – to Participation.**3, 112**
Bowyer, Donna.............................**126p.**
Boys' School................................**72, 80**
Braun, Eric....................................**90, 99**
Browndale Treatment Centre..............**80**
Building a Framework For Support.....**89**
By Ourselves.......................................**92**
CAC (Consumer Advisory Committee)
    .................................................**94pp.**
Calder Centre....................................**106**
Calvert, Lorne.....................................**99**

Canada Assistance Plan.......................**64**
Canadian Charter of Rights and
    Freedoms.......................................**15**
CAO (Children's Advocate Office).**106p.**
Carment, Laura...........................**4, 79p.**
CBO (Community-based Organization
    ...........................................**11p., 130p.**
CCF (Cooperative Commonwealth
    Federation)...............................**43, 46**
CELDIC (Commission on Emotional
    and Learning Disorders in Canada)
    .................................................**76, 84**
Chapman, James..................................**75**
Children's Services Policy Framework
    ......................................................**105**
Church, Kathryn.........................**37, 88p.**
CIHI (Canadian Institute for Health
    Information)..................................**108**
Clancy, Ian...................................**33, 41**
Clarke, C.K. ...............................**17, 23**
Coates, Lloyd C..................................**73**
College of Physicians and Surgeons.**46p.**
Come Together consumer group, Moose
    Jaw..............................................**126**
Commission on Medicare..................**100**
Commission on the Future of Health
    Care in Canada ............................**100**
Community Mental Health Action:
    Primary Prevention Programming in
    Canada...........................................**87**
Community Reinvestment:  Balancing
    the Use of Resources to Support
    People with Mental Disabilities......89
Community Resource Base................**88**

Community School......................**81, 105**
Community Services Branch..............**78**
Compulsive Gambling Education........**97**
Consumer Participation:  From Concept
  to Reality .......................................**89**
Conway, John (U of S)....................**129p.**
Crocus Coop.............**15, 90, 94, 115, 124**
Dafoe, Ruth...................................**98**
Dale's House...............................**72, 106**
Davidson, Agnes (Mrs. R. J.).......**27, 30,
  41p., 105**
Davidson, Larry.............................**116p.**
Denson, Ray...................................**72**
Disability Action Plan.......................**99**
DISC  (Disability Income Support
  Coalition)......................................**101**
Douglas, T. C................................**43pp.**
Downton, Darrell............................**126p.**
Dyck, Ted.......................................**3, 121**
ECIP (Early Childhood Intervention
  Programs)......................................**79**
ECT (Electro-Convulsive Treatment). .**64**
Educational Psychologist.....................**71**
Embury House................................**73p.**
EPI (Early Psychosis Intervention)....**104**
Epp, Jake.......................................**92**
Estevan..........................................**38, 40**
Evans, Barbara..............................**94, 96**
Evergreen: A Child and Youth Mental
  Health Framework for Canada......**135**
FAC (Family Advisory Committee). **93p.**
FASD (Fetal Alcohol Spectrum
  Disorder).......................................**79**
Forgotten Constituents..**9, 82pp., 93, 106**
Fountain House........................**59p., 62**
Framework for Support. .**88, 90, 92, 117,
  132**
Frazier, Shervert..........................**69p., 83**
Free Spirit Band................................**120**
Friends for Life..........................**97, 127**
From Consumer to Citizen..................**89**
FROMI (Friends and Relatives of the
  Mentally Ill)....................................**93**
Fyke, Kenneth J. provincial Commission
  on Medicare...................................**100**
Garnet, Stephen.................................**89**
Gathercole, Frederick J......................**69**

Gondziola, Arthur...............................**91**
Gorecki, Donna..................................**98**
Greenough, Tim..................................**81**
Griffith, J.D.M....................................**24**
Grunberg, Frederic..............................**46**
Harman, Joyce..............................**56, 61**
Healing through Humour...................**121**
Henbury, Lewis A...............................**45**
Hill, Lynn...........................................**3**
Hincks, Clarence.................**19p., 23, 43**
Histoire Sociale/ Social History............**3**
Hoffer, Abram.............**20p., 46p., 66pp.**
Home and School Association........**24p.**
Hospital Insurance and Diagnostic
  Services Act....................................**46**
Hylton, John.......................................**94**
Iceberg on the Horizon...................**3, 111**
Improving the Health of Canadians 2008
  .......................................................**108**
Institute of Child Guidance and
  Development....................................**75**
Izumi, Kyo (Kioshi)......................**21, 47**
Jaksa, B.............................................**56**
Jaques, Hazel......................................**19**
Just Having Fun Harmony Group......**120**
Kahan, Irwin J.................**35, 53, 60, 67p.**
Keegan, David....................................**95**
Keon, Wilbert J.................................**132**
Keyes, Marjorie............................**19, 23**
KidsFirst...........................................**103**
Kilburn Hall.......................................**72**
Kinar, Doug.......................................**122**
Kindersley.....................**11, 63, 97, 115**
Kinsmen Club.....................................**56**
Kirby, Michael J...............................**132**
Knowledge Exchange Centre.............**134**
Lafave, Hugh......................................**79**
Lawson, Sam....................**44, 46p., 49**
Laycock, Sam..............................**24, 75**
Leader..............................................**46**
Life Long Learning Centre (formerly
  Seniors' Education Centre)................**3**
Line, W..............................................**24**
Lipscombe, Colin................................**81**
Lloyd, Woodrow.................................**47**
Lloydminster......................................**63**
Low, David.........................................**17**

Lutcher, Donna......................................**94**
Maclean's magazine...........................**109**
MacLeod, John.....................................**75**
MacNeill Clinic....**66, 72, 74, 78, 81, 103**
MacNeill, James Walter.................**18, 20**
Mahon, John........................................**74**
Maple Creek........................................**46**
Marris, Eve...........................**35, 38, 41**
Mayotte, A. S......................................**51**
McDonald, Ian.........................**9, 83, 106**
McKerracher, D. G. "Griff"...**20, 25, 44,
    46, 64, 73, 124**
McKinnon, Fred A...............................**71**
McNeil, Don........................................**78**
Medicare.....................**46p., 60, 63, 100**
Melfort...............................................**63**
Mental Health Act...........................**43, 63**
Mental Health Coalition.....**91, 100, 102,
    127, 136p.**
Mental Health First Aid.............**127, 133**
Mental Health for Canadians:  Striking a
    Balance...........................................**92**
Mental Health Sector Study...............**130**
Mental Health Services Act.................**96**
MHCC (Mental Health Commission of
    Canada)...........**16, 127p., 132pp., 137**
Millar, David.......................................**95**
Moose Jaw.**11, 43, 64, 67, 80p., 97, 119,
    121, 126**
Morrison, Ian.....................................**121**
Morrison, L.A......................................**69**
National Crime Prevention Strategy..**103**
National Film Board............................**25**
NCAC (National Consumer Advisory
    Committee)................................**89, 95**
NDP (New Democratic Party).......**46, 99**
Nelson, Dave...................................**3, 129**
NGO (Non-government organization). **11**
Niro, June............................................**93**
North Battleford **9, 17pp., 25, 27, 30, 41,
    43, 52, 56, 59, 63p., 102**
O'Connor, Phyllis .................................**3**
One Million Children............................**76**
Osmond, Humphrey. .**20p., 27, 30p., 35,
    37p., 40p., 45**
OT (Occupational Therapy)...**19, 31, 33,
    35, 49, 52**

Out of the Shadows...........................**132**
PAC (Professional Advisory Committee)
    ................................................**93pp.**
Pape, Bonnie......................................**89**
Parley, Kay..................................**33, 39**
Partners Against Violence.................**126**
Partners for Mental Health...............**133**
Patient First.............................**128, 135**
Pawson, Geoff....................................**74**
Pepper, Betty......................................**91**
Phillips, Jo Anne..............................**104**
PIND (Provincial Interagency Network
    on Disability)......................**98, 101p.**
Prince Albert **11, 15, 27, 29, 45, 55p., 64,
    68, 79, 91, 94p., 97, 106, 115,
    119pp., 124**
Privacy Act....................................**4, 136**
Pruden, Beverly..................................**46**
PSB (Psychiatric Services Branch)....**20,
    25, 44, 47, 52, 55, 64pp., 69p., 75,
    78p., 84**
Public Health Nurses..........................**71**
Quance, Frank M................................**24**
Rainbow Youth Centre........................**75**
Ranch Ehrlo Society......**74, 76, 104, 107**
Randall, David.............................**80, 105**
Recovery..............**3, 13, 90, 115pp., 124**
Red Willow Centre............................**106**
Regina.**2p., 5, 11, 15, 19, 27, 29p., 33p.,
    37pp., 43pp., 51p., 56, 60, 64p.,
    72pp., 77, 80, 92, 94pp., 99, 103pp.,
    109, 115pp., 122, 131, 136p.**
Regina Association for Children with
    Learning Disabilities.......................**75**
Regina Child and Youth Mental Health
    Services...........................................**75**
Regina Reel Anti-Suppressants..........**120**
Riddell, Art.........................................**27**
RN (Registered Nurses).......................**80**
Rohn, George...............................**44, 52**
Romanow, Roy ............................**100p.**
Rotary Club.........................................**56**
RPNAS (Registered Psychiatric Nurses
    Association of Saskatchewan). .**3, 102**
RPNs （Registered Psychiatric
    Nurses）.....................................**78, 80**
RQHR (Regina Qu'Appelle Health

Region)......................................**103p.**
Rundval, Arlen...................................**94**
Russell, Terry................**3p., 75pp., 79p.**
SACL (Sask Association for Community
    Living)................**68, 79, 96, 101, 136**
SAID (Sask Assured Income for
    Disability)..................................**101p.**
Saskatchewan Arts Board..................**121**
Saskatchewan Association for Retarded
    Children...........................................**68**
Saskatchewan Parks and Recreation
    Association...............................**3, 125**
Saskatchewan Plan....**43p., 46p., 52, 64,
    69, 83, 91, 132**
Saskatchewan Prescription Drug Plan. **97**
Saskatchewan Seniors Mechanism........**3**
Saskatchewan Tourism, Parks, Culture
    and Sport......................................**3**
Saskatchewan Training School............**67**
Saskatchewan Transportation Company
    ...................................................**29**
Saskatoon..**2p., 9, 11, 15, 19, 24, 27, 29,
    41, 43pp., 47, 52, 55pp., 61, 64, 66p.,
    69, 71pp., 77p., 80p., 90, 93pp.,
    103p., 106, 108p., 115, 119, 121pp.,
    131**
Saskatoon Health Region...**103, 109, 125**
SCDI (Sask Council on Disability
    Issues)...........................................**98p.**
Schizophrenia Society..................**98, 136**
SchoolPLUS.....................................**105**
Schultz, Rose...................................**36p.**
Scott, Bob.........................................**80**
Scott, Walter......................................**17**
Secord, Doris......................................**23**
Shaping Mental Health Policy: An
    Action Agenda for Canada..............**89**
SHARE (Self-Help and Recreation /
    Education) Prince Albert...**91, 94, 115**
Shaunavon.........................................**46**
SHNB (Sask Hospital North Battleford)
    ...........................**17p., 20, 52, 55, 102**
SHW (Sask Hospital Weyburn)..........18

Sigerist, Henry...................................**43**
Smith, Colin M............................**64, 79**
Sommer, Robert...........................**28, 37**
Special Report on Rehabilitation of
    Handicapped Persons in
    Saskatchewan................................**58**
SPI (Saskatchewan Prevention Institute)
    .......................................................**79**
STEP parenting...................................**75**
Stephen, Alexander....................**66, 72p.**
Stewart, A..........................................**69**
Stotz, Sandy...................................**122pp.**
Strom, Rob.......................................**109**
Swift Current........**11, 46, 52, 56, 64, 80,
    119pp.**
Thatcher, Ross....................................**63**
The Club.....................................**15, 120**
The Nest......................................**15, 120**
The School Act....................................**77**
Toews, John.........................................**87**
Toombs, N. M..............................**44, 52**
Toward Recovery and Wellbeing: A
    Framework...................................**132**
Trainor, John......................................**88**
Transition magazine.............**93, 119, 121**
Treherne, Dave...................................**81**
Turanski, James..................................**80**
Tymchak, Michael.............................**105**
Ulysses Plan.......................................**97**
United Way.......................................**125**
Valley View Centre.............................**80**
Vogt, Mary.........................................**28**
Volunteer Saskatoon.......................**122p.**
Wadsworth, Joan................................**38**
Wall, Brad........................................**102**
Wascana Institute...............................**78**
Weyburn...**3, 11, 18pp., 25, 27pp., 33p.,
    36, 38pp., 46p., 51p., 56, 59, 63p.,
    67, 69, 80, 97, 115, 119pp.**
World Health Organization.................**13**
Y.E.S. (Youth Employment Services). .**76**
Yorkton..........**11, 46p., 64, 78, 80, 95, 97**
Young Offenders Act .........................**80**

# ENDNOTES

1 *Histoire Sociale/ Social History* XLIV:88, University of Ottawa, November 2011, pp. 287-304.

2 CMHA (Sask). *A Recovery / Resiliency Plan for Mental Health & Addictions in Saskatchewan*. Regina: September 2008, p 5.

3 These people would have been settlers. Research on Aboriginal mental health services, historically and presently, is beyond the scope of this history.

4 F. H. Kahan, *Brains and Bricks: The History of Yorkton Psychiatric Centre*. Regina: White Cross Publication, CMHA (Sask), 1965, pp. 13-16. Note: Mrs. Fannie H. Kahan, journalist, was the wife of Irwin J. Kahan, executive director of CMHA Saskatchewan. This book tells a more complete story of the people and politics behind the Yorkton Centre

5 "Mental Health Services." *The Encyclopedia of Saskatchewan*. http://esask.uregina.ca/entry/mental_health_services.html accessed August 18, 2012.

6 *Under the Dome: The Life and Times of Saskatchewan Hospital Weyburn*. Weyburn, Souris Valley History Book Committee (1986), p. 3.

7 Terry Russell, *Growing Pains: The Development of Children's Mental Health Services in Saskatchewan*. ms. Chapter 1, p. 6. Early copy of ms. received electronically by chapters, no page numbers.

8 John D. Griffin. *In Search of Sanity: A Chronicle of the Canadian Mental Health Association 1918 – 1988;* London, Canada: Third Eye, 1989, p. 27.

9 CMHA (Sask) *The Forgotten Constituents: A Report on the Task Force Committee on the Mental Health Services in Saskatchewan*. Regina: Mental Health Association in Saskatchewan, May 1983, p. 15

10 Harley D Dickinson. *The Two Psychiatries: The Transformation of Psychiatric Work in Saskatchewan 1905-1984*. Regina: Canadian Plains Research Centre, U of Regina, 1989, pp. 79-81.

11 *The Forgotten Constituents,* p 16-17.

12 Erika Dyck.. *Psychedelic Psychiatry: LSD on the Canadian Prairies*. Winnipeg: University of Manitoba Press, 2012.

13 F.H.,Kahan,, pp. 41-76.

14 CMHA National. *History of CMHA*. http://www.cmha.ca/about-cmha/history-of-cmha/ accessed July 12, 2012.

15 Ramdhawa Bikkers and Dennis Hunt, "More on Psychology in Saskatchewan", *The Saskatchewan Psychologist* 84: 4, Nov 1984.

16 A.D. Treherne, "Educational Psychology in Saskatchewan: A Review of its History and Current Directions." *Sask Psychologist* 84:2, May 1984.

17 Russell, ms. Chapter 3, p. 2.

18 N. M. Agnew, "History of the SPA: A Small Biased Sample by a Founding Member." *Sask Psychologist,* May 1966.

19 Griffin, p. 155.

20 Kathleen Kendall,. "From Closed Ranks to Open Doors: Elaine and John Cummings' Mental Health Education Experiment in 1950s Saskatchewan," *Histoire Social/ Social History* XLIV: 88, November 2011, p. 261.

21 Griffin, p. 166.

22 Griffin, p. 208; *The Forgotten Constituents*, p. 17.

23 Further research is required to document the beginning of the volunteer visiting program at North Battleford. Gratitude is extended to Mrs. R.J. Davidson, volunteer coordinator for CMHA (Saskatchewan) who kept careful records. Special thanks to Phyllis O'Connor, Executive Secretary of CMHA Saskatchewan, who compiled a binder of these notes in 2005.

24 This paper focuses on the Weyburn program but recognizes the work and dedication of the volunteers to SHNB.

25 SAB R1265 IV.A.92, Osmond correspondence (January 12, 1960). The report listed the names of organizations who had participated and celebrated 27 individuals who had received pins for 100 hours or more of volunteer services in the first eight years of the program Volunteer service was the time spent visiting, not the time spent travelling. Osmond's recollection is different than F. H. Kahan recorded in *The History of the Saskatchewan Volunteer* (1960?) also in SAB R1265 IV.A.92 which said "The first six volunteers to Weyburn were Mrs. Lloyd Coates, Mrs. E.W. Larrigan, Mrs. R.J. Davidson, Mrs. Floyd Dixon, Mrs. George Wright, and Dr. B. C. Campden-Main, psychiatrist with the Munroe Wing."

26 Ray Belanger. "Therapies (1923-81)" in *Under the Dome: The Life and Times of Saskatchewan Hospital, Weyburn*. Weyburn, Souris Valley History Book Committee (1986).

27 *Under the Dome,* p. 63.

28 *Under the Dome,* p. 63.

29 Kay Parley. *Lady with a Lantern*, Regina: Benchmark Press (2007), p. 10.

30 R1265 II.A.8 Brief to Government 1956-57 80-469.

31 SAB R1265 II.A.77 Volunteer Work, 1958. Osmond, H. "Correspondence" February 21, 1957.

32 Schultz, Rose, personal interview, Weyburn, Jan. 26, 2009.

33 *Under the Dome*, p. 8.

34 *Under the Dome*, p. 196.

35 SAB R1265 II.A.77 Volunteer Work, 1958. Davidson, Agnes, "Report prepared for National Newsletter", October 6, 1958.

36 *Under the Dome*, p. 21.

37 Soo Line Historical Museum, Weyburn, Saskatchewan: "Open Door Policy" Slide 146 of 231.

38 Soo Line Historical Museum: "Interview with Elsie Postet & Mary Konotopetz (December 07, 2007) slide 228 of 231 accessed August 18, 012 http://www.virtualmuseum.ca/pm_v2.php? id=record_detail&fl=0&lg=English&ex=363&hs=0&rd=92458 .

39 Parley, 194-196.

40 *Weyburn Review,* December 24, 1964 "Regina CMHA visitors brave stormy weather" from CMHA Volunteer Visiting binder.

41 John H. Archer, *Saskatchewan: A History.* Saskatoon: Saskatchewan Archives Board, Western Producer Prairie Books, 1980, p. 262.

42 SAB R1265, CMHA Saskatchewan Papers, IV.A.92. D. G. McKerracher,

"Some Aspects of Psychiatric Development", n.d.

43 Gregory P. Marchildon. "A House Divided: Deinstitutionalization, Medicare and the Canadian Mental Health Association in Saskatchewan, 1944-1964." *Histoire Sociale / Social History* XLIV: 88, November 2011, p. 311.

44 Marchildon, p 311.

45 *The Forgotten Constituents,* pp. 11-13.

46 Marchildon, p, 316.

47 McKerracher, n.d.

48 Marchildon, p. 317

49 SAB, R1265 II.A.8 Brief to Government 1956-57 The rod and carrot refers to an old story that offers two ways to get a donkey moving, with a stick to its back or a carrot on a stick in front of it.

50 SAB R1265 11.A.8 Brief to Government 1956-57 file, a yellow carbon copy of the Letter to the Editor.

51 SAB R1265 II.A.8 Brief to Government 1956-57, Lewis A. Henbury, Division office confidential letter to Dr. H.. Osmond, Superintendent, SHW dated July 18, 1957

52 Marchildon, p 319-320.

53 Marchildon, p. 320-322.

54 Kahan, F.H., 1965, p.35.

55 F.H. Kahan, 1965, p 131.

56 Marchildon, p. 325-326.

57 Marchildon, p. 326-327.

58 *The Forgotten Constituents,* p. 19.

59 SAB R1265 IV.A.92 Irwin Kahan – Articles 1960-1962 reprinted as a handout by CMHA from *Regina Leader Post,* January 29,1960.

60 SAB R1265 IV.A. 92 Irwin Kahan.

61 SAB R1265 II.A. 8 CMHA Brief to Government 1956-57. *Some of the Social Worker's Functions and Problems in Initiating a Rehabilitation Program,* n.d.

62 SAB R1265 II.A.83 CMHA Newsletters, Nov 1957 and May 1960, Kahan "Somewhere to Go"

63 SAB R1265 II.A.8 Brief to Government 1956-57.

64 SAB R1265 II.A.82 CMHA Saskatchewan Division Newsletter #1, October 1958.

65 SAB R1265 IV.A. 92 Irwin Kahan.

66 SAB R1265 IV.A.92 Irwin Kahan.

67 SAB R1265 IV.A. 92 Irwin Kahan.

68 RR1265 II.A.83 CMHA Newsletters, Nov 1957 and May 1960, Kahan "Somewhere to Go."

69 RR1265 II.A.83 CMHA Newsletters, Nov 1957.

70 RR1265 II.A.83 "Somewhere to Go."

71 SAB R1265 II.H.5 White Cross Centre Reports, 1960-1961.

72 SAB R1265 II.H.3. CMHA Divisional Rehabilitation Committee, minutes, February 1958, October 22, 1958, February 28, 1961, March 28, 1960.

73 SAB R1265 II.H.5 White Cross, 1960-1961. Jaksa, B., "Recommendation for White Cross Centres", April 1960.

74 SAB R1265 II.H.5 White Cross, 1960-1961.

75 SAB R1265 II.H.5 White Cross, 1960-1961. "Duties of the White Cross Centre Director."

76 SAB R1265 II.H.5 White Cross, 1960-1961. "Duties."

77 SAB R1265 II.H.3. CMHA Saskatchewan Division minutes, October 12-13, 1960; SAB R1265 II.H.4 Minutes Divisional White Cross Centre Committee meeting, February 28, 1961.

78 The Saskatchewan Council for Crippled Children and Adults, the Canadian Arthritis and Rheumatism Society, the Saskatchewan Association for Retarded Children, the Canadian National Institute for the Blind, and CMHA

79 SAB R1265 IV.A.53 Provincial Coordinator of Rehabilitation of Disabled Persons, *Special Report on Rehabilitation of Handicapped Persons in Saskatchewan* for Presentation to Advisory Planning Committee on Medical Care, July 1960, pp. 8-10.

80 SAB R1265 IV.A.53 Rehabilitation Council, 1960. Office of the Provincial Coordinator of Rehabilitation, *Rehabilitation of the Handicapped in Saskatchewan Newsletter*, Regina, March 1960, p. 2. Also announced in this newsletter was proposed construction of the Yorkton "Community Psychiatric Centre", p.1.

81 SAB R1265 IV.A.53 Provincial Coordinator, *Special Report*, pp 1-2.

82 SAB R1265 IV.A.53 Rehabilitation Council, 1960.

83 SAB R1265 IV.A.53 Rehabilitation Council, 1960, p.3.

84 SAB R1265 IV.A.53 Rehabilitation Council, 1960, p. 9.

85 SAB R1265 IV.A.53 Rehabilitation Council, 1960, p.3.

86 SAB R1265 II.H.4 Divisional White Cross Centre Committee Minutes 1961.

87 SAB R1265 II.H.4 Divisional White Cross Centre Committee Minutes 1961.

88 Rehabilitation Council, March 1960, newsletter. Other positions and salaries included Psychiatric Social Worker II for Moose Jaw Union Hospital at a salary of $379-$461 per month and a Psychiatric Social Worker for Psychiatric Services Branch at $350 to $426 per month with classifications of Psychologists from $350 to $606 per month.

89 John H. Beard, Rudyard N. Propst, and Thomas J. Malamud, "The Fountain House Model of Psychiatric Rehabilitation" in *Psychosocial Rehabilitation Journal* V:1, January 1982.

90 SAB R1265 IV.A.92 Irwin Kahan – Articles 1960-1962. "Somewhere to Go."

91 SAB R1265 II.H.4 Divisional White Cross Centre Committee Minutes 1961, August 1961.

92 SAB R1265 II.H.4  Minutes 1961, August 1961.

93 Griffin, pp 174-75

94 William A Anthony. *Rehabilitation Programs in the 1980s: Laying the Groundwork for the 1990s.* Boston University: Center for Psychiatric Rehabilitation. Paper presented at the Twelfth Mary Switzer Memorial Seminar, June, 1988, pp. 2-3. Accessed in CMHA (Sask) library.

95 SAB R1265 V.D.2 Annual Meeting 1964. Dr. Colin M. Smith, "Medical Action for Mental Health"

96 Anonymous. "Life in mental hospital reviewed", *Regina Leader-Post*, January 20, 1960.

97 SAB R1265 V.B.3.

98 SAB R1265 V.B.4 Minutes of Special Advisory Committee, January 3, 1968 at University of Saskatchewan.

99 SAB R1265 V.B.4 Special Advisory.

100 SAB R1265 V.D.2 Annual Meeting 1964: Minutes of January 3, 1968 signed by F. J. S. Esher, M.D., Department of Psychiatry, Jan 18, 1968.

101 James Sanheim, "Community Support for People with Intellectual Disabilities." *The Encyclopedia of Saskatchewan,* accessed August 18, 2012.
http://esask.uregina.ca/entry/community_support_for_people_with_intellectual_disabilities.html

102 SAB R1265 V. Scientific Planning Committee 1968. Kahan memo dated 2/9/66, p. 4.

103 SAB R1265 V.B.4  Advisory SPC 1968. Letter to Mrs. A. M. Derby, President, CMHA from Dr. Hoffer, M.D., Ph.D. dated September 9, 1968.

104 Frazier, Shervert H. and Alex D. Pokorny, *Report of a Consultation to the Minister of Public Health on the Psychiatric Services of Saskatchewan,* Regina: Government of Sask, 1968, p. 26-27.

105 Frazier, 1968, p. 6.

106 Frazier, 1968,

107 Dooley, Chris, "The End of the Asylum (Town): Community responses to the depopulation and closure of the Saskatchewan Hospital, Weyburn" *Histoire Sociale / Social History* XLIV: 88, Nov 2011, p.349

108 Frazier, 1986, p 19.

109 Frazier, 1986, p. 25.

110 *The Forgotten Constituents,* p. 22-23.

111 Russell, ms. chapter 3

112 Frazier, 1968, pp 36-37.

113 Russell, ms. chapter 3, p.2.

114 SAB S347, Stephen Papers. F. A. McKinnon brief to Subcommittee on Services to Emotionally Disturbed Children.

115 Tim Greenough, Executive Director, MacNeill Clinic, Saskatoon, interview, Oct. 14, 2010.

116 SAB S81-18, Saskatoon, "Papers of Dr. Alexander Stephen",

117 Carment, Laura, email communication, January 22, 2011.

118 Russell, ms, chapter 3, p. 7.

119 SAB S347, Alexander Stephen, "For Canadian Conference on Children, 1960, Facilities for the Treatment of Emotionally Disturbed Children in Saskatchewan."

120 Lobb, Harold, "Profile of Nelson Abraham," The *Sask Psychologist*, May, 1955.

121 SAB S81-18 Stephen papers, clipping, no date, no publication named.

122 Ranch Ehrlo, "Founder and History" http://www.ehrlo.com/about-us/mission-vision-and-culture/founder-history/ accessed August 18, 2012.

123 G. J. Pawson, *Ranch Ehrlo: Home for Emotionally Disturbed Children.* SAB, Stephen Papers, S347. I.91. Pawson was the executive director of Ranch Ehrlo.

124 Margaret Blair. "MacNeill Clinic and Saskatoon Mental Health Clinic", *The Sask Psychologist* 74:4, November 1974, pp. 26-27.

125 SAB, Saskatoon, S81-18 Papers of Dr. Alexander Stephen, *Seminar on Child Psychiatry* at the U. of S. October.1965.

126 Russell, ms. ms. chapters 4, 5 and 6 recorded the history of the Regina Child and Youth Mental Health.

127 Russell, ms. chapter 6, "The Early Philosophical Basis of Regina Child and Youth Services."

128 Peterson, Gladys, "The Summer at Harding House," *Sask Psychologist*, 74:3, August 1974.

129 Russell, ms. chapter 6, pp. 2-3 "The Early Philosophical Basis of Regina Child and Youth Services"

130 Russell, ms, chapter 3, p. 7 "Child Welfare."

131 Laycock, S. R. (reviewer), "*One Million Children*",*Canadian Counsellor*, Vol 4:4, October 1970 at University of Calgary 2418-8812-1-PB[1].pdf accessed July 8, 2012.

132 Russell, ms., chapter 3, p.3.

133 Russell, ms., chapter 3, p.7.

134 Carment, Laura, phone interview December 16, 2010. Carment, a social worker with Regina Child and Youth served as the first Psychiatric Services Branch Director for Children and Youth Mental Health.

135 McNeil, Don, "Youth Services at Yorkton Psychiatric Centre." *Sask Psychologist*,74;4, November 1974, pp. 21-22.

136 Early Childhood Intervention Program, *Toy Box Angels: A Collection of ECIP Family Stories*, Regina: 2007, p,8-16: "Excerpts taken from the *Operational Review of Saskatchewan's ECIPs Appendix A: ECIP Sask. Inc.—Historical Review* by Nicole R. Wohlgmuth and Janet Mantler, June 2005.

137 Government of Saskatchewan/ Education / Early Childhood Education/ History accessed August 18, 2012 http://www.education.gov.sk.ca/Default.aspx?DN=68462090-5800-4c92-8537-989dc3417265 .

138 Russell, ms. chapter 4, p.4

139 Carment, interview.

140 Saskatchewan Prevention Institute "Early Childhood Mental Health" accessed Aug 18, 2012 http://www.preventioninstitute.sk.ca/early-childhood-mental-health .

141 Saskatchewan Health Services for People with Disabilities "Fetal Alcohol Spectrum Disorder" http://www.health.gov.sk.ca/fetal-alcohol-spectrum accessed November 12, 2011.

142 FASD Support Network of Saskatchewan Inc. http://www.skfasnetwork.ca/About%20Us.html accessed November 12, 2011.

143 Carment, interview.

144 Russell, ms. Chapter 4

145 Saskatchewan Community Schools Association (SCCA), "History and Mandate" http://www.communityschools.ca/aboutus-ourhistory.html accessed Aug 18, 2012. Horsman, Ken. *Education.* "SchoolPlus" http://esask.uregina.ca/entry/education.html *Encyclopedia of Saskatchewan* accessed August 1, 2012.

146 A. D. Treherne. "Educational Psychology in Saskatchewan: A Review of its History and Current Directions", *Sask Psychologist* 84:2, May 1984. The next issue of the journal reported Treherne's death on September 5, 1984.

147 *The Saskatchewan Psychologist* 84:4, November 1984.

148 Treherne.

149 *The Forgotten Constituents, p. 1.*

150 *The Forgotten Constituents,* p. 7.

151 *The Forgotten Constituents,* p. 7.

152 *The Forgotten Constituents,* p.7-8.

153 The Commission on Emotional and Learning Disorders in Children (CELDIC), *One Million Children*, Toronto, 1970. See review by Dr. S. R. Laycock, *Canadian Counsellor,* Vol 4:4, October 1970 at University of Calgary 2418-8812-1-PB[1].pdf accessed July 8, 2012.

154 *The Forgotten Consituents*, ,p. 88-91.

155 *The Forgotten Constituents,* pp.5-6.

156 *The Forgotten Constituents,* p. 24.

157 D. Paul Lumsden (editor), "On Assessing and Ameliorating the 'Costs' of Social Life" in *Community Mental Health Action: Primary Prevention Programming in Canada* for the Primary Prevention Committee of CMHA, Ottawa: The Canadian Public Health Association, 1984, pp. 1-18.

158 Lumsden.

159 CMHA National, *Framework for Support: Third Edition,* Toronto, 2004, graphic used with permission.

160 Bonnie Pape. *Shaping Mental Health Policy: An Action Agenda for Canada.* Toronto: Canadian Mental Health Association, National Office, October 1987, p. 5.

161 Kathryn Church. *From Consumer to Citizen.* Toronto: CMHA National,1986.

162 John Trainor, Ed Pomeroy and Bonnie Pape *A Framework for Support:*

*Third Edition* CMHA National,  CMHA National, Toronto, 2004.

163 Ed. Holgate. *Involvement of Consumers in Saskatchewan* for Board meeting, January 6, 1985.

164 CMHA 69th Annual Conference Program. Saskatoon: September 1987.

165 CMHA (Sask) file 500.2 Mental Health Coalition 1986 – 1989. Letter from Garry Molitwenik, Executive Director of SHARE, Prince Albert to Eric Braun, President of Crocus Coop, Saskatoon dated December 11, 1986 following up on a December 2nd meeting.

166 CMHA (Sask) 500.2.  Press Release January 15, 1988.

167 CMHA (Sask) 500.2, Press Release January 15, 1988.

168 CMHA (Sask) 500.2   Letter from Bob Hughes, Coordinator on By Ourselves letterhead to Garry Molitwenik, Co-Chairperson of the Mental Health Steering Committee dated December 14, 1988.

169 Pape (1987) *Shaping Mental Health Policy:   An Action Agenda for Canada.*

170 June Niro,"President's Report" Annual meeting, June 12, 1988, Yorkton, p. 2.

171 David Keegan :A Report of the Professional Advisory Committee to the Board of the Saskatchewan Mental Health Association, December 3, 1988. in *CMHA (Sask Div) Annual Reports 1974/75 to 1988/89* binder at Division office. Members were Dean Ian McDonald, College of Medicine, U of S; Professor Norma Stewart, Nursing Research Professor, U of S; Dr. Tim Greenough, Director at MacNeill Clinic, Saskatoon; Mr. Glenn Rutherford, social worker and Director of Cosmopolitan Industries sheltered workshop; Professor Wilber Nelson, Theologian and Pastoral Care Coordinator, U of S; Mr. Gerald Albright, a lawyer; and Mrs. Byrna Barclay, a family member and writer from Regina.

172 CMHA (Sask) Annual Meeting, April 30, 1989, Moose Jaw, "President's Report."

173 CMHA (Sask) *Transition*, Regina: 1989.

174 CMHA (Sask) Annual Meeting, April 30, 1989, Moose Jaw, "Executive Director's Report".

175 CMHA (Sask) 1990/91 Annual Report  B*uilding the Dream, CAC Report.*

176 CMHA (Sask) 1990/91 Annual Report.

177 CMHA (Sask) 1990/91 Byrna Barclay, President's Report.

178 CMHA (Sask) *1992-93 Strategic Plan*, Regina, April 1992, in binder *CMHA(Sask Division Annual Reports 1989/90 – 2005/06.*

179 CMHA (Sask) 1992/93 Annual Report, *Into the Era of Health Reform.*

180 CMHA (Sask) 1993/94 Annual Report, Executive Director's Report.

181 Dagnone, Tony   *For Patients' Sake:   Patient First Review Commissioner's Report to the Saskatchewan Minister of Health,* Regina,  October 2009.   p.46.   http://www.health.gov.sk.ca/patient-first-commissioners-report accessed July 31, 2012.

182 CMHA (Sask) 1994/95 Annual Report, President's Report. 1995/96 Executive Director's Report. 1997/98 Executive Directors Report.

183 CMHA (Sask) .Annual reports, 1997-98, 1988-99.

184 British Columbia Schizophrenia Society, *Ulysses Agreement*, http://www.bcss.org/wp-content/uploads/Ulysses-Agreement-blank-adult.pdf accessed July 11, 2012.

185 CMHA (Sask), Annual Meeting 1994/95, CAC Report.

186 CMHA (Sask) PIND 1995-2001 Minutes and Agenda.

187 CMHA (Sask) PIND 995-2001 Miscellaneous, "Draft To Ministers of Post Secondary Education & Social Services." Fax from Michael Huck to John Hylton, Jan. 31, 1996, p. 8

188 CMHA (Sask) PIND Minutes and Agendas, PIND Minutes, June 20, 2001.

189 Saskatchewan Council on Disability Issues (SCDI), *Saskatchewan's Disability Action Plan*, Regina, June 2001. http://www.philia.ca/files/pdf/sask.pdf accessed Aug 5, 2012, p. 57

190 Ruth Dafoe, a retired social worker, represented the Saskatchewan Schizophrenia Society.

191 SCDI, p. 6.

192 SCDI, pp. 13-16.

193 SCDI, pp. 25-54.

194 Kenneth J Fyke. *Caring for Medicare: Sustaining a Quality System.* Government of Saskatchewan, Regina, April 2001, p.82.

195 A. Pirisi, 2000. "Mental Health Vies for Attention" , *The Lancet* 356: 9245, p. 1908 quoted in Fyke, p. 16.

196 Fyke, p. 16.

197 Fyke, , pp. 1-5.

198 Roy J. Romanow. *Building on Values: The Future of Health Care in Canada, Commission on the Future of Health Care in Canada*, Ottawa, November 2002

199 Romanow, p. xvii.

200 Romanow, p. xxxi and 178-179.

201 Romanow, p. 179.

202 CMHA (Sask) 600.4 DISC 2005-1007

203 CMHA (Sask) *2011-2012 Annual Report*, "Community Partnerships", p. 9-10.

204 Government of Sask, Press Release, *Background Information: Saskatchewan Hospital North Battleford Building Replacement Project.* Regina: August 18, 2011. http://www.gov.sk.ca/adx/aspx/adxGetMedia.aspx? mediaId=1519&PN=Shared accessed Aug 20, 2012.

205 Government of Sask, Education, *KidsFirst*, http://www.education.gov.sk.ca/KidsFirst accessed Aug. 13. 2012.

206 Horsman,Ken, "Education - SchoolPLUS" *Encyclopedia of Saskatchewan*, http://esask.uregina.ca/entry/education.html accessed Aug. 18, 2012.

207 Canadian Institute for Health Information (CIHI) *Improving the Health

*of Canadians 2008:  Mental Health, Delinquency and Criminal Activity*, Ottawa: 2008, p. 21

208 Ranch Ehrlo. "Mission, Vision and Culture http://www.ehrlo.com/about-us/mission-vision-and-culture/    accessed November 28, 2011.

209 Regina Qu'Appelle Health Region *Health News*, Winter 1999, pp. 1, 6.

210 *Dorland's Illustrated Medical Dictionary,* "psychosis", p. 1573

211 Elizabeth Lines, *Canadian Early Psychosis Initiatives*, Toronto: CMHA National,    March    2001,    http://www.cmha.ca/data/1/rec_docs/ 163_canadian_inititatives.pdf accessed Aug 18, 2012.

212 Saskatchewan Community Schools Association. "CommunityEducation." http://www.communityschools.ca/aboutus-ourhistory.html    accessed Aug. 18, 2012.

213 Saskatchewan Learning, *Children's Services Policy Framework*, Regina, 2002.

214 Sask Learning, Children's Services and Programs Branch.  *Building Communities of Hope:  Best Practices for Meeting the Learning Needs of At-Risk and    Indian    and    Métis    Students.*    Regina:    2004,    p.1. http://www.education.gov.sk.ca/building-communities-of-hope accessed Aug 18, 2012.

215 Saskatchewan Health, *Regional Health Authority Community Program Profile,* October 2006, pp. 38-42.

216 Saskatchewan Youth in Care and Custody Network Inc.,  *Rights & Responsibilities:  A Handbook for Youth in Care,* Regina (n.d.) , p.6. www.syiccn.ca  accessed November 17, 2011.

217 Saskatoon Health Region  "Child and Youth Residential" accessed Aug 18,    2012    http://www.saskatoonhealthregion.ca/your_health/ps_mhas_ child_and_youth_residential.html

218   Children's Advocate Office (CAO) *It's Time for a Plan for Children's Mental Health,*  Regina, April 2004.

219 CAO 2004.

220 CAO 2004, p.6.

221  CAO 2004, p. 80

222  Saskatchewan Health, Community Care Branch, *Regional Health Authority Community Program Profile*, October 2006.

223 Saskatchewan Health, *A Better Future for Youth:  Saskatchewan's Plan for Child and Youth Mental Health Services*, Regina, (2006).

224 Canadian Institute for Health Information (CIHI) published *Improving the Health of Canadians 2008:  Mental Health, Delinquency and Criminal Activity*, Ottawa, 2008, p. 4.

225 CIHI quoting Statistics Canada National Longitudinal Survey of Children and Youth (NLSCY), pp 24, 10-11.

226 CIHI, pp. 15-20.

227 CIHI, p. 21.

228 CIHI, pp. 40-41.

229 Ken MacQueen and Julia Belluz. "Mental Health for the Few." *Maclean's,* March 28, 2011.

230 Saskatoon Parent Education Committee, *The Incredible Parent Directory 2009/2010.*
*http://www.saskatoonhealthregion.ca/pdf/Incredible_Parent_Directory_All.pdf*
accessed July 5, 2012.

231 CMHA (Sask) and Jayne Melville Whyte, *Iceberg on the Horizon: Mental Health among Older Adults: Social, Intellectual, Spiritual,* (MH-OASIS), Regina, March 2004.

232 *Iceberg,* (p.40).

233 CMHA (Sask) and Jayne Melville Whyte, *Beyond Barriers – To Participation: Recreation for older adults with mental illness.* Regina, June 2010.

234 Federal, Provincial and Territorial Committee of Officials (Seniors), *Healthy aging in Canada: a new vision, a vital investment. From Evidence to Action* (Background Paper), Ottawa. 2006.

235 CMHA (Sask) and Jayne Melville Whyte, *Setting Goals and Building Capacity: A Recovery Model for CMHA Social Recreation in Saskatchewan.* Regina: June 2011. This whole chapter is based on the visits to Branches, surveys, and telephone conversations from this project.

236 CMHA (Sask) and Schizophrenia Society of Saskatchewan, *Life Beyond Illness: The move towards recovery,* Annual Conference, Regina, June 12-14, 2008.

237 Davidson, Larry. *How to transform a system to recovery without really trying (or at least without having to do all the hard work yourself).* PowerPoint™, 2008

238 Davidson, *How to transform.*

239 Davidson, Larry *How to transform.* PowerPoint™, 2008

240 CMHA Regina Annual Report 2009-2010

241 Ted Dyck, "Writing for Your Life: Mid-term Report" in *Transition,* Spring 2012. Regina: CMHA.

242 CMHA (Sask) "Retreat 2002 Presentation Outline", p. 24.

243 CMHA (Sask) Retreat 2002, p. 23.

244 John Conway, (U. of S.) *Saskatchewan Mental Health Sector Study Final Report* prepared for the Mental Health Workforce in Saskatchewan, funded by Saskatchewan Learning in partnership with Saskatchewan Health, Regina, January 2003.

245 Conway, 2003, pp. 8-13.

246 Conway, 2003, p. 13..

247 Conway, 2003, p. 14.

248 Conway, 2003, p. 37.

249 CMHA (Sask). *Mental Health Sector Study: Value of the Direct Voice - The Role of Community Based Organizations in Delivering and Improving Mental Health Services in Saskatchewan* prepared by Innova Learning, Regina, August 2007, p. 4.

250 CMHA (Sask) 2007, *Mental Health Sector*, p. 30-31.

251 CMHA (Sask) 2007, *Mental Health Sector*, p. 32-36.

252 Michael J. L Kirby and Wilbert Joseph Keon, *Out of the Shadows at Last: Transforming Mental Health, Mental Illness and Addiction Services in Canada.* Final Report of The Standing Senate Committee on Social Affairs, Science and Technology, Ottawa, May 2006.

253 Trainor et al. *A Framework for Support: Third Edition.* Ottawa: CMHA National 2004.

254 Kirby, 2006, p. 435-436.

255 Mental Health Commission of Canada, News from MHCC, Child and Youth Special Edition, p. 7 http://www.mentalhealthcommission.ca/ SiteCollectionDocuments/Newsletters/MHHC_Newsletter_Sept2011_ENG.pdf .

256 S. Kutcher and A. McLuckie for the Child and Youth Advisory Committee, Mental Health Commission of Cananda (2010). *Evergreen: A child and youth mental health framework for Canada.* Calgary, AB. Mental Health Commission of Canada.

257 Kutcher, *Evergreen:* p. 17.

258 Dagnone, Tony. *Patient First* 2009. p.3. http://www.health.gov.sk.ca/patient-first-commissioners-report

259 Dagnone, pp. 6-7.

260 Dagnone, p. 45.

261 Dagnone, p. 55.

262 Praxis Consulting. *A Call to Action – A Collaborative Mental Wellbeing Strategy for Regina and Area,* 2012, p.4 http://www.praxis-consulting.ca/wellbeingstrategy/_pdfs/Mental_Wellbeing_Strategy.pdf accessed August 24, 2012.

263 *A Call to Action,* pp. 12-14.

264 Mental Health Commission of Canada. *On Our Way* brochure, http://www.mentalhealthcommission.ca/SiteCollectionDocuments/brochures/Refer ences%20for%20On%20Our%20Way%20map.pdf accessed July 14, 2012.

265 Peter Coleridge. *Building Collective Impact.* PowerPoint to CMHA (Sask) AGM, June 22, 2012.